50 A$KS

in 50 Weeks

A Guide to Better Fundraising for Your Small Development Shop

Amy M. Eisenstein, MPA, CFRE

50 A$KS

in 50 Weeks

A Guide to Better Fundraising for Your Small Development Shop

50 Asks in 50 Weeks: A Guide to Better Fundraising for Your Small Development Shop
One of the **In the Trenches**™ series
Published by
CharityChannel Press, an imprint of CharityChannel LLC
30021 Tomas, Suite 300
Rancho Santa Margarita, CA 92688-2128 USA

www.charitychannel.com

ISBN: 978-0-9841580-2-7
Library of Congress Control Number: 2010928003

13 12 11 10   8 7 6 5 4 3 2 1

Printed in the United States of America

This and most CharityChannel Press books are available at special quantity discounts for bulk purchases for sales promotions, premiums, fundraising, or educational use.

About the Author

Amy M. Eisenstein

Amy M. Eisenstein, MPA, CFRE, is the principal and owner of Tri Point Fundraising, a full-service consulting firm for nonprofit organizations and foundations. Her firm serves a wide variety of social service, educational and healthcare organizations.

Before creating Tri Point Fundraising, Amy served for more than ten years in the nonprofit sector as a director of development for large and small nonprofit organizations. These include the New Jersey Institute for Social Justice, the Associate Alumnae of Douglass College at Rutgers University, and Shelter Our Sisters, a battered-women's shelter. For these organizations she raised millions of dollars through event planning, grant writing, capital campaigns, direct mail as well as major and planned gift solicitations.

Amy is a frequent speaker at conferences and a facilitator of board retreats. She currently serves on the board of the Association of Fundraising Professionals – New Jersey Chapter and is chair of the 2010 New Jersey Conference on Philanthropy. She received her Master's Degree in Public Administration and Nonprofit Management from the Wagner Graduate School at New York University and her Bachelor's Degree from Douglass College at Rutgers University.

Acknowledgements

Many thanks to my friends and colleagues at the New Jersey Chapter of the Association of Fundraising Professionals. AFP-NJ has provided me with quality ongoing education over the last decade and is where I learned "the basics" at the beginning of my career.

My appreciation also goes to Brenda Hebert, Michelle Wilson, Gene Wilk, Ray Brush, Monica Reiss, Arnie Edelstein, Jackie Brendel, Elizabeth Gloeggler, Jean Stockdale, Arlene Correa, Cathy Proctor and Dan Meyler for your suggestions and guidance. And a special thanks to Dawn Knill, my personal *50 Asks* cheerleader.

Thank you to Stephen Nill, Founder and CEO of CharityChannel, for recognizing raw talent and taking a chance on a first-time author. I appreciate your patience and good humor.

I would like to thank Elaine Meyerson, the first person to hire me when I knew nothing about fundraising in my first one-person development shop.

An extra special thanks to my mentor, hero and friend, Mark Valli.

And finally, but most importantly, I would like to express my heartfelt gratitude to my family and friends who have supported me and my career over the years, especially my parents, sister, my husband Alan and our children Ethan and Zoe.

Amy M. Eisenstein, MPA, CFRE

Contents

Foreword

I've been a fundraiser for a long time and have read my share of fundraising books. So why write a foreword for this one?

For starters, Amy's enthusiasm for fundraising and the people and programs that benefit is palpable and contagious, and she brings a fresh and innovative approach to development planning in her very first book.

50 Asks in 50 Weeks is an easy and worthwhile read for busy professionals, especially those in smaller development shops, because it provides a structured, diverse and realistic array of practical tips for boosting your fundraising revenue. It will help any nonprofit executive director or development staff member jumpstart their fundraising efforts by returning to the basics, but basics at their best and most efficient.

I commend Amy for getting us back to basics and creating this book as a tool to reach those who may be newer to the profession of fundraising or those who do not have extensive staff or training budgets. This valuable resource is a must-have for anyone thinking of starting a new fundraising program, individuals who are new to the field of development, and those who want to refresh and refocus their efforts. For those who have been in a small development shop for many years, it will provide reassurance, reminders of best practices, encouragement and a renewal of passion and enthusiasm for the work you do.

The planning tools and concepts outlined in *50 Asks in 50 Weeks* demonstrate how to raise more money without using additional resources. The keys to your success will be to structure your actions so you ask more frequently, diversify your funding base, and be smarter about your fundraising efforts. Each chapter takes an in-depth look at one element of the fundraising planning process and provides practical tips and hints along with way. The to-do lists, charts and calendars are tangible resources to guide you along the way.

I concur with Amy's assessment of small development offices and her advice for them. Her helpful hints and practical suggestions are right on point. I am pleased to write the foreword for this book and support Amy's efforts.

Roberta (Robbe) Healey, MBA, NHA, ACFRE
Chair
Board of Directors
Association of Fundraising Professionals

Introduction

I n 1998, I hated fundraising. I had visions of cold calls and clammy hands. At that time, I was in graduate school at NYU, studying public administration and nonprofit management.

However, I knew one thing: I wanted to be an executive director of a nonprofit. I knew that if I was to rise through the ranks of any nonprofit I would need to either fundraise or supervise fundraisers. What I didn't quite understand then is that an integral part of being an executive director IS fundraising.

I thought I needed to get fundraising experience "out of the way," so I applied for my first fundraising job as a first step toward nonprofit leadership. Much to my surprise I loved it and fell in love with fundraising!

Today you couldn't pay me enough to be an executive director, and you couldn't tear me away from fundraising. Nonprofits live and die (or muddle along) on their fundraising abilities, or lack thereof, which means that fundraising successes determine the fate of the organization. I cannot imagine a bigger thrill than successfully closing a gift and knowing that I am part of the reason that the good work of an important organization can continue.

I hope by the end of this book you will love fundraising too (or at least understand it better and feel more comfortable doing it). Fundraising is NOT begging for money; it is helping people to invest in important causes. As a development staff member, executive director or volunteer, when you raise funds for a cause, you are helping donors invest in something that is important to them, to you and to society. Whether the issue is education, homelessness, the environment, healthcare, the elderly, children, people with disabilities or a host of other worthy, important causes, you're involved in the solution when you raise funds.

So let's get fundraising...

There are many reasons why nonprofit organizations do not raise as much as they could (or should). One is that many fundraisers, executive directors and board members don't actively fundraise. They passively sit waiting for the phone to ring or wait for someone else to do it. Fundraising is a lot of work and takes a team of people working together to get the job done.

Another reason that nonprofits don't raise as much as they could is that "asking for gifts" often falls to the bottom of a long list of urgent but ultimately less important work. Even experienced fundraisers can get sidetracked with other tasks such as planning events, writing grant reports, newsletters and thank you letters, managing databases, and updating websites. While extremely important, these tasks do not lead directly to any additional income for the organization. In fact, asking needs to be moved back to the top of the priority list.

The first time I had to "ask" was in my first fundraising job at a battered women's shelter. The organization had very little money to pay a fundraiser, so it took someone with no fundraising experience (me) and relied on the fact that other life experiences, education and enthusiasm would pay off.

This "back to basics" book is meant to serve as a guide for fundraisers and executive directors who feel stuck or unsure about their fundraising abilities or results. It is also a fantastic resource for those who are just entering the world of fundraising. Executive directors will especially benefit from Chapter Seven.

Regardless of your specific fundraising role, the information in this book will help you to diversify your funding base, ask for donations in smarter, more efficient ways, and most importantly, emphasize the importance of asking frequently. At the end, you will have the ability to create a twelve-month development plan that will include a list of fifty prospective funders for your organization plus an action plan of how (and when) to ask for gifts.

It's simple but true: You don't and won't get gifts without asking. I know that sounds obvious, but I also know many smart, hard-working fundraisers who get so caught up in day-to-day tasks they actually forget to "ask."

While there are many critical components of a small development office, you cannot raise money if you do not ask for gifts. The following pages are about getting back to basics, increasing the number and size of gifts you ask for and receive, and keeping you disciplined so you remember to "ask" all year long.

> An **ask** is the actual solicitation in the fundraising process. I will use the term to refer to any request for money, including a grant application, event invitation, appeal letter, sponsorship request or an individual, face-to-face solicitation.

One of the primary culprits in low fundraising revenue for nonprofits is low "ask" numbers and amounts. What I mean by this is that when you ask too infrequently, you won't raise as much as you could by asking more. Additionally, many fundraisers ask for too little money when they do ask. Ask for more money each time you ask.

Beyond frequency, we will discuss "smart" asking because frequency is not the only factor. Quantity without quality will not lead to success.

Most people are scared the first few times they get involved with fundraising, and many organizations lack the resources to do things perfectly. But once you start asking more frequently, you will find that it is not as daunting as it first appeared. And, the resulting increased donations will catapult you into an upward spiral. So stop with the excuses and get asking!

Once you realize how infrequently you are asking for donations, asking more often will be an obvious way to raise more money. If you are already making more than fifty smart, diverse asks per year, how many more could you make?

By the end of this book, you will be able to create a smarter and more diversified plan for raising funds. You will have the ability to identify new sources of potential funding and therefore will not be dependent on any one entity. Finally, you will have additional tools and techniques to solicit

A **prospect** is an individual, foundation or corporation that has been identified as a potential donor to your organization.

Identification is the first stage of the fundraising cycle. This is the stage where prospective donors are identified.

Cultivation is a process where prospects and organizations get to know one another. In other words, board and staff members educate prospects about the organization and get to know the prospect. Cultivation takes place over a period of time and can last from a few months to several years prior to asking for a gift.

Solicitation is the actual ask and is what most people think of when they hear about fundraising. Solicitation generally lasts for only one moment in time, as opposed to the rest of the fundraising process. Solicitations can happen in person, by mail, by application or by phone.

Stewardship is the thanking or follow-up stage. After a gift is made, it is important to properly steward donors.

funds from foundations, corporations and individuals. Your organization will be much more stable, wealthy and thrilled with you!

This book is about jumpstarting your small development office, which means raising more money for your organization, getting energized and excited, and getting back on track!

Fifty is a somewhat arbitrary number, but with approximately one ask per week, it fits nicely into a year. Also, I have found that most small nonprofits (with one or no development staff members) are not making fifty asks per year. No matter how many asks you are currently making, the concept of 50 Asks in 50 Weeks is designed to get you asking more frequently and more efficiently in addition to helping you diversify your funding base.

Throughout the book you will find worksheets to help you plan your 50 Asks in 50 Weeks. Take time to fill them out as you go through the book, and then use them for the next year. If you do, I am certain that you will raise more money for your organization!

This book is divided into sections, including five chapters that the major solicitation sub-categories fall into: board members, bulk solicitations, individuals, foundations and events (or sponsorships). There is also a chapter dedicated to executive directors and hiring and working with development staff.

Chapter One introduces the concept of 50 Asks in 50 Weeks in more detail. It covers how to count your asks, so you have a benchmark against which to measure yourself. You will also learn why having a diverse funding base and asking "smart" are both critical for success.

Chapter Two details the roles and responsibilities of the board with regard to fundraising. I explain why it is necessary to have 100 percent participation by board members, and what it means for them to give and get donations. The chapter ends with a brief list of suggestions for getting your board more involved in fundraising.

Chapters Three through Six review the major categories of fundraising (bulk mail, individuals, grants and events) and will provide detailed ideas for adding asks to your calendar in each category.

Chapter Seven is geared specifically for executive directors. It covers the role of the executive director and the role's relationship with the board and fundraising staff. The chapter concludes with an in depth look at how and when to hire a first development staff member.

Chapter Eight wraps things up by reviewing goal setting and creating action steps to ensure success.

There are sidebars throughout the book that will help draw your attention to:

◆ Stories from the Real World
◆ Helpful Hints
◆ Definitions
◆ Counting Your Asks
◆ To Do Lists

Charts and tables throughout will help you organize your asks, as well as create benchmarks and a goal for your number of asks.

This book is specifically designed to help organizations make a huge leap in their fundraising income—not difficult once you realize that you are not asking for gifts nearly as often as you could be.

Once you have put your plan into action, I urge you to contact me with the results: both successes and setbacks. Let me know what has worked well for you and what has not.

You can download all charts found in this book from my website at www.tripointfundraising.com.

Best wishes for your fundraising success!

Amy M. Eisenstein, MPA, CFRE
Tri Point Fundraising
(201) 970-9766
amy@tripointfundraising.com
www.tripointfundraising.com
Twitter: @amyeisenstein

Chapter One

Getting Started: What You Need to Know

IN THIS CHAPTER

- ┈▶ Why everyone at your organization is a fundraiser

- ┈▶ Defining and counting your asks

- ┈▶ Why frequency, diversity and efficiency are critical to success

- ┈▶ Making a case for support for your organization

- ┈▶ The fundraising cycle: Identification, Cultivation, Solicitation and Stewardship

In this Chapter the concept of 50 Asks in 50 Weeks will be explained in greater detail. I will discuss the importance of having a baseline of asks; in other words, knowing how many asks you are currently making and how much money you are raising. This is important so that you are able to measure your future success. You will also learn the system I use to count asks. Included in this chapter are definitions of basic fundraising concepts: identification, cultivation, solicitation and stewardship, which will be used throughout the remainder of this book.

Frequency Counts: How Many Asks Are You Making?

Paying more attention to the frequency of asking is important because most nonprofit organizations are not making as many asks as they could (or should) yet wonder why they are not raising enough money. Pointing a spotlight on the number of asks you are making throughout the year will create an easy benchmark to see if you are getting more asks out the door each subsequent year.

Many nonprofits are only asking twenty to thirty times per year (or fewer) using the counting method outlined in this book. If your organization is like most small nonprofits, I assume that it is not receiving all the gifts you ask for (most organizations do not have 100 percent success rates). If you are receiving every gift you ask for, then you are certainly not asking frequently enough or for enough money from each request. If you are not getting all the gifts you ask for, then you are likely receiving far fewer than fifty gifts per year.

Those organizations with fundraisers (executive directors, staff and board members) who are actively involved in fundraising, not stuck behind their desks doing paperwork but out in the community building relationships, will be the most successful fundraisers in any economy.

In a nonprofit organization, fundraising is EVERYONE'S responsibility, including the person answering the phone, program staff, the executive director and all board members. It is important for all staff members and volunteers to have some fundraising training and awareness, not just the development staff.

On a daily basis, though, fundraising is primarily the responsibility of the executive director and fundraising staff, with help from the board. For you executive directors: Even if you have a fundraising staff, it is still your responsibility to identify, cultivate, solicit and steward your donors on an ongoing basis.

At the end of this section there are worksheets that will help you list your asks for counting purposes and future reference. In order to increase the number of asks you make in the future, you will first need to know how many you are currently making.

Definitions of "Asks" for the Purpose of Counting

1 bulk mail appeal = 1 ask
Regardless of whether you are mailing to 50, 500, or 5,000, this includes event invitations, appeal letters, newsletters with business reply envelopes and e-mails with clear requests for funding.

1 individual request = 1 ask
Asking an individual for a specific amount for a specific project or purpose.

1 grant proposal (application) = 1 ask
Addressing a funder's specific guidelines, not a generic application or letter.

1 sponsorship solicitation = 1 ask
Solicitation is specific to that prospect, not simply changing the name and address at the top of a letter, preferably with a personal contact (e-mail, phone call, etc.) from someone who knows the recipient of the letter or someone at the company.

The Importance of a Diverse Funding Base

Another key to a successful small development program, whether it is run by a single fundraising professional, the executive director or members of the board, is to ensure a diversified funding base. This means having a variety of sources of income to your organization.

A well balanced portfolio of donors is crucial to the safety and financial security of any nonprofit. Your organization should have a variety of

A **diversified funding base** is having multiple revenue streams coming from a variety of sources.

finition

donors in each of the following areas: foundations, corporations, individuals and government support (at the federal, state, or local level).

The reason that a diverse funding base is so critically important is that organizations that rely on single sources of income put themselves, their programs, and the people they serve in jeopardy in the event that any funding source is eliminated.

Another reason to have a diverse funding base is that most funders do not want to be the lone supporter of an entire program or organization. This is true for a variety of reasons, including:

◆ Funders want to be able to spread their resources around a variety of organizations, and not spend all their funding on one agency.

◆ Funders do not want a program (or agency) to be completely dependent on their dollars. The more funders that support a particular organization, the less likely a program is to disappear if one funder stops funding it.

◆ Funders do not want to take big risks. They feel more comfortable when they join others in supporting a particular program.

On the same note, funders do not want to invest their money in a "sinking ship." It's important to be confident in your organization and not come off as desperate. No one wants to "save" your agency.

The story in the Stories from the Real World sidebar is just one example of a nonprofit relying too heavily on a single funding source, such as government funding or a private grant. If you follow the 50 Asks in 50 Weeks plan, you can help ensure that your organization receives funding from a wide variety of sources and will remain stable in spite of potential funding cuts.

I once worked for an organization where the largest program was funded by a single donor. The program trained urban, low-income, young adults to become apprentices for construction trade unions. Although I expressed concern about the stability of the program due to its being funded by a single source, I was told to not worry. The fact was that the funder used our program as an example of a model program and truly loved the program. However, when the funder changed its funding criteria a few years later, the program was not refunded. If the program had been funded by at least one other source, we might have had six months or so to look for alternate funding. Unfortunately, because we had relied on a single source of funding for the program, when it was suddenly and unexpectedly cut, there was nothing we could do except cancel the program for the following year.

stories from the real world

Asking Smart

The old saying "quality not quantity" rings true in the fundraising context. It is more important to make smart, informed asks than to make a certain number of asks each year. So although increasing the overall number of asks your organization is making is crucial, it is not enough. Prospective donors, whether foundations, corporations or individuals, must be carefully researched, cultivated, solicited and stewarded.

If you ask one hundred times per year, but do not receive any gifts, then frequency becomes irrelevant. It is actually the number of gifts you receive, not the number of gifts you ask for, that truly counts. Your requests must be of high quality to truly ensure success.

The following story in the Stories from the Real World sidebar gives an example of unproductive fundraising. In place of the Valentine's card sale we instituted three new ideas that raised the profile of the shelter in the community and raised many more dollars, without too much additional effort.

When I started working at a battered-women's shelter, one of the first projects I was asked to work on was a Valentine's Day card sale. It was an annual fundraiser at the shelter where board members and other volunteers sold Valentine's Day cards at busy train stations around the area. The shelter only netted a few dollars per box, yet a tremendous amount of energy and volunteer time was used to sell each box. We were primarily selling the cards for cash to people who would never be added to our mailing list and who probably did not know about or care much about the cause. It was too little return for too much work. Unfortunately the board and staff had been so reliant on the small infusion of unrestricted cash it brought in each winter that they were extremely reluctant to give it up.

Here are some examples of improvements we made at the shelter after eliminating the Valentine's Day card sale:

◆ We created a newsletter with a business reply envelope. We received about ten back and each envelope had an average of $50, which meant we raised $500 while at the same time raising awareness about our programs. (Subsequent newsletters continued to raise more money.) While $500 is a small amount of money, it was an investment in our future individual giving program. Those mailings helped us identify potential larger donors for the future, and started getting people in the habit of writing checks to the shelter on a somewhat regular basis.

◆ We implemented a sponsorship program for the annual dinner. In addition to selling tickets to our annual dinner, we created sponsorship levels at $1,000, $2,500, and $5,000. The first year we got one of each! It was $8,500 dollars plus thirty new people (three tables) at the dinner that we had never had before.

◆ We added a silent auction component to the dinner, which raised almost $10,000.

Implementing these new development strategies was much smarter fundraising than the card sale, and for the amount of effort required, yielded much greater results. After that successful year, the board and staff were happy to give up the Valentine's Day card sale.

Do you have any fundraising events that do not earn the amount of money they should for the amount of effort required? (I specifically say *fundraising* events here because organizations have lots of other reasons for having events—such as publicity/community awareness/cultivation events, which are not fundraising events and should not be expected to raise money.)

Think carefully about the difference between these events. Some organizations charge a "fee for service" to cover their costs for these events, but find that it is difficult to ask for a donation on top of that fee because people feel as if they have already donated— even if the cost of the event actually only covered their meal and other expenses.

Look carefully at revenue versus expenses for your events and appeals, including staff and volunteer time. Once you evaluate your events, you might discover some that need cutting, or you might be able to identify opportunities to make your efforts more efficient and effective. Also consider completely eliminating some events in exchange for alternative activities that are likely to yield more revenue with less time and effort. One of the ways to raise more money this year is to make sure you are making the best use of your time.

Making a Case for Support

A case statement is a written document that conveys the important work of the organization and is an argument as to why the organization deserves donations. It is important to be able to communicate the mission of the organization passionately and succinctly. The case for support, which is often called a "case statement," is the pitch for giving.

It is important to have a written case statement so that you have a document to provide to donors and prospective donors that explains your organization in both a detailed and succinct way.

It might be helpful to your staff and board members if you provide a wallet-sized card with bullet points and statistics for them to have on hand about your organization. In general, however, I hate scripted "elevator speeches," because I can never remember them when I need them.

A **case statement** is a written statement about why your organization is important, worthy and deserves donations.

finition

On the other hand, in addition to a written case for support, I believe that it is equally as important that staff and board members are able to talk passionately about the organization. Although this particular message will not be consistent throughout the organization, it will be personal, meaningful and very persuasive, if done right. While this might seem easy and obvious, it actually is quite difficult for most people and takes practice.

To practice this at a board meeting or retreat, have each participant (board and staff members) think about what attracted them to the organization, and why they continue to be involved. After a few minutes ask everyone to stand up and pair off. The pairs should tell each other in two to three minutes why they are involved and what they love about the organization. Once each person has had a chance to tell their story, they switch partners. Do this until everyone has spoken to everyone else or all have told their story between five and ten times. With every telling, each story gets more concise and articulate. Board members learn about each other and why each of them joined. It is a very powerful experience, especially for those who might not feel as connected to the cause. Each participant is now prepared to go out into the community and tell these same stories to friends, neighbors, colleagues and other prospective donors at cocktail parties, in the grocery store, or at work.

This is not a "formal" or written case for support, but it effectively gets the message across. As you probably know, people give to people, not just to organizations or causes. This personal perspective is extremely powerful in recruiting friends and donors to your organization.

Have you heard the "80/20 rule" that 20 percent of your donors give 80 percent of your dollars? In many cases, it is actually only your top 10 percent of donors giving your organization 90 percent of the funds raised. Find out what the ratio is at your organization and pay most attention to those top donors. You might find that you were spending 90 percent of your time with the bottom donors, who were only contributing 10 percent of the dollars raised. You should be focusing most of your time on your top 10 percent of donors, who contribute 90 percent of the dollars raised.

Understanding Fundraising From Start to Finish

There are four stages of fundraising that apply to all prospects. I will discuss each stage in detail throughout the coming chapters as they apply to each type of fundraising activity or prospect. The stages are:

1. **Identification**—identifying prospects, that is, potential donors.

2. **Cultivation**—the "getting to know you" stage for the organization and prospect.

3. **Solicitation**—the "ask" or request for funds.

4. **Stewardship**—follow-up and thank you.

The fundraising cycle is important for executive directors, board members and development staff to understand. All participants have an important role to play at each stage.

Fundraising Cycle

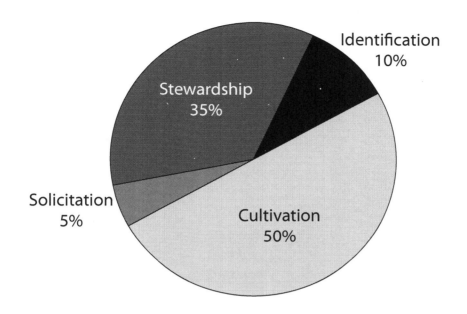

I created this pie chart to illustrate my experience with the fundraising cycle. The pie represents the amount of time it takes for an organization to identify a prospect, cultivate the prospect, solicit a gift, and steward the gift, regardless of whether the process takes a month, a year or several years.

When board members and executive directors say they do not want to fundraise, most are referring to the ask, or solicitation, stage. As this graph shows, the solicitation is only one moment in time (5 percent) in a much longer process. Most people are willing to get involved in the identification, cultivation and stewardship stages.

Creating a Baseline and Counting Your Asks

Use the following charts to count the number of asks you currently make each year. You can use the last twelve calendar months or the last fiscal or calendar year. It does not matter what twelve months you use as long as

List Current Asks: Grant Applications

Year: _____

	Foundation/Corporation Name	Amount Requested/Received	Due Date
Example	XYZ Foundation	$15,000 Requested/$10,000 Received	
1			
2			
3			
4			
5			

TOTAL REQUESTED: $ _____

TOTAL RECEIVED: $ _____

List Current Asks: Individuals (Face-to-Face Solicitations)

Year: _____

Name	Amount Requested/Received
Example *Mrs. Donor*	*$10,000 Requested/$6,500 Received*
1	
2	
3	
4	
5	

TOTAL REQUESTED: $ _____

TOTAL RECEIVED: $ _____

List Current Asks: Sponsors

Year: _____

	Sponsor Name Individual or Corporations	Event Name (Golf or Gala)	Amount Requested/Amount Received
Example	XYZ Company	Spring Gala	$5,000 Requested $5,000 Received
1			
2			
3			
4			
5			

TOTAL REQUESTED: $ _____

TOTAL RECEIVED: $ _____

List Current Asks: Bulk Solicitations

Year: _____

	Name/Description	Number Mailed/ Number Donors	Total Raised	Date Sent
Example	Spring Appeal	1500 Mailed 120 Donors	$4,500 Raised	March 10
1				
2				
3				
4				
5				

TOTAL REQUESTED: $ _____

TOTAL RECEIVED: $ _____

Counting Asks Summary (All Solicitation Types)

Year: _____

Solicitations	Number of Asks Made	Number of Gifts Made	Notes
100% Board Participation			
Grants			
Individuals			
Sponsors			
Bulk			
Other			
TOTAL			

you are consistent in your comparisons.
To Recap

◆ Make more asks to raise more money.

◆ Diversify your funding base for a financially stable organization.

◆ Make smart asks—efficiency and frequency are important, but asks without gifts are meaningless.

◆ A solid case for support is critical for success.

◆ The fundraising cycle has four stages: identification, cultivation, solicitation and stewardship.

Chapter Two

Board Members are Fundraisers

IN THIS CHAPTER

···➔ Board members and their financial responsibility

···➔ Achieving 100 percent participation from your board

···➔ Boosting board giving to your organization

···➔ Ways to get your board members involved with fundraising

I n this chapter I will discuss board member roles and responsibilities with regard to fundraising. Board members are responsible for making their own contribution (giving to the organization) and for helping to raise funds (getting). It is up to you to help educate your board members so that they understand their role and feel comfortable doing it. I have provided some suggestions to get board members involved at all stages of the fundraising cycle, as well as ongoing and periodic activities for them.

Roles and Responsibilities

While we love and value our volunteer board members, I often hear complaints from executive directors and development staff that board members are not doing their job, mostly with regard to fundraising. One of the primary reasons that board members do not serve their organizations well is that we as staff have not adequately prepared them for the job. We need to provide a comprehensive job description, an orientation session including a tour and materials, and ongoing training and support.

Only when we have done our due diligence and properly informed, oriented, and trained board members can we consider proper action for removing underperforming board members.

The board has two primary responsibilities: governance and fundraising. Governance is generally the more popular function of board members and includes setting policies and procedures, overseeing investments and the budgeting process, and making sure the organization fulfills its mission. Contrary to the belief of many board members, they are not responsible for the daily management of the organization. Day-to-day management is the responsibility of the staff, overseen by the executive director. One of the board's primary management functions is to hire, fire, and evaluate the executive director.

After being adequately trained, you might still have board members who only want to govern and not contribute financially or help raise funds. I find it useful to remind reluctant board members that there will not be an organization to govern if adequate funds are not raised. When having this candid discussion, have a list of alternate volunteer opportunities available to suggest in the event that they decide that the board is not the right place for them.

Although governing is an essential responsibility for board members, for our purposes I am going to focus on board member responsibilities as donors and fundraisers.

Give and Get

If you have board members who think the act of showing up for board meetings a few times per year is their "gift" to the organization, you have not done a good job of recruiting or educating them. When dealing with these board members, you should take the opportunity to teach them about their important role with the organization, and if they still do not make a personal contribution and help raise funds, they can be asked to step down and take another volunteer position with the organization.

Do you know the traditional expression "give or get"? By the way, I think give AND get is better. The phrase, however you say it, refers to board members, and it means give money, (and) get money, or get off the board.

This diagram represents your organization, with the board and staff as the innermost circle. Donors and supporters are the next closest people to your organization. Finally, the outermost circle represents the community at large, those who live or work in your community and could be converted into donors or supporters of the organization. When fundraising, always start with the innermost circle and work your way out.

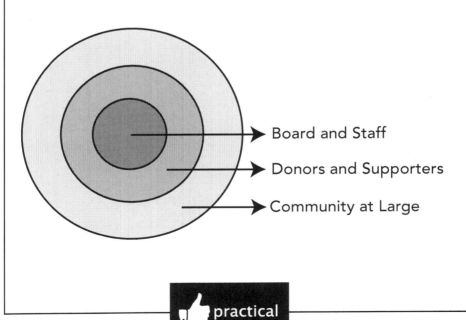

Board and Staff

Donors and Supporters

Community at Large

practical tip

Why use such a strong phrase? If board members who are the closest to the organization, and therefore have the most intimate knowledge of the organization's needs, are not giving, why should others? In other words, the board is the innermost circle of the organization, and if board members do not feel compelled to give, it is going to be very hard to convince others to do so.

Board members should be the first persons asked to give a donation (gift) to your organization each year, and they should be the first to make their annual commitments. Board members are expected to contribute and "kick off" any campaign (annual or capital).

Here are some questions to ask yourself when thinking about your board and fundraising:

◆ Is your entire board giving? If not, why not?

◆ Have board members been asked to make a gift? (Not asked as a group, but *individually* asked?)

◆ Have board members been asked to help fundraise? Have they been given the training, guidance and tools to be successful?

One Hundred Percent Participation and Board Giving

One hundred percent participation means that everyone on the board writes a personal check. This is essential for future fundraising success. If board members, who are part of your organization's innermost circle, won't give, why would anyone else? Many more foundations and savvy individual donors are asking organizations about board giving before making

> **One hundred percent participation** refers to your board and the number of board members who are giving to your organization. *All* board members must contribute.

I recently worked with an organization that applied to a foundation that required 100 percent participation of board members. The executive director was honest in telling the foundation that there was one board member who did not give. The foundation refused to consider a grant until the following year, when there was 100 percent participation.

Only after he cost them a grant did the board member fully understand the implications of his actions. He finally wrote a check.

a gift decision. Having 100 percent board participation means that your board members are truly committed to the cause.

If board members have been individually asked to give and still have not given, they either need a reminder ask or to be asked to step off the board.

If there is a non-donating member of your board who is your star volunteer, then you should schedule a private conversation between that person and yourself or the board president. Explain that any gift, no matter how small, will be greatly appreciated and is expected of all board members.

I do not know of any working persons who serve on a board who cannot give one hundred dollars. You can let them do quarterly payments of twenty-five dollars per quarter, if necessary. If they are still unwilling, you can let them know that they are putting future funding in jeopardy and that you are going to ask them to step off the board and into another volunteer position. Of course, do so graciously and let them know how much you appreciate their work for the organization.

One great (and easy) way to turn over your board is to enforce term limits. This will help you remove long-serving board members who might no longer understand the direction your organization is heading. You can also institute a board member "review" at the end of each year and ask some tough questions such as:

◆ *Do you (as a board member) feel you were able to serve the organization as well as you could have?*

◆ *Did you advocate for, give personally, and raise funds for the organization this year?*

◆ *Do you wish to continue to serve?*

In addition to the expectation of 100 percent participation, some boards implement a minimum give or get amount. This means that board members are expected to give or raise (or any combination thereof) a minimum, pre-set amount.

While this approach does set a clear expectation, I am not a supporter of mandatory minimum gifts. I believe that a minimum gift floor can easily become the ceiling. For example, if you require a board member to give a minimum of $1,000, two things can happen:

1. All board members who are able will give $1,000—even the ones who have the capacity to give more, and,

2. Hardworking, loyal board members who do not have the capacity to give $1,000 will drop off the board.

Instead of mandatory amounts, I like to encourage each board member to make a stretch gift. This means that each board member should make a gift that is large for the member's own

---

A **stretch gift** is a gift of any amount that is large for that particular donor's giving ability. When a person is considering a stretch gift, it is a contribution that requires serious thinking before giving, and not one that can easily be made. It is often a gift of a sizeable enough amount that the donor would discuss it with a spouse or family member prior to making the gift.

finition

I was leading a board retreat recently and a board member admitted to giving significantly more to her church than to the organization where she served on the board. She lumped in the charity, of which she was sitting on the board, with the rest of her charitable giving—about $100 per year to each of ten or so other charities. Once she understood that board members were asked to make the organization one of their top priorities, she immediately increased her annual gift from $100 per year to $2000—still not as much as she was giving to her church, but significantly more than she was giving to any other charity. And it was a stretch gift for her.

stories from the real world

budget, which will ultimately result in a larger total board gift than would a mandatory minimum gift level.

Easy Methods to Boost Board Giving

Provide Quarterly or Monthly Payment Plans

Many board members can significantly increase their giving if you can provide a monthly or quarterly payment option. Some examples are:

◆ A board member who gives $150 annually might be willing to give $50 per quarter instead. If so, the member will increase the gift by 25 percent to $200 annually.

◆ A board member who gives $500 annually might be willing to give $100 per month, for a total gift of $1,200, which would increase their gift by more than 50 percent!

The key here is to have the capacity to accept credit cards and do the monthly or quarterly charging without bothering the board member each time. This way you are not reliant on board members remembering to write monthly checks. Be sure you don't lose money because you are unable to collect pledge payments.

Asking your board counts as your first ask for the year. Add it to your list of 50 Asks at the end of this book.

counting your asks

Expect to be in the "Top Three"

Ask board members to create a confidential list of their annual giving, including names of the charities that they give to and the amounts. This list is for their eyes only. Tell them that as board members you expect a "stretch" gift from them, which means it should be a large gift for their budget. Their gift to your charity should be one of the top three gifts they make this year.

Provide a Challenge or Matching Gift Opportunity

A board member, individual, or company can provide a challenge gift to your organization and structure it so that each board member must participate in order to receive the challenge gift. For example, a board member could pledge $10,000 if the rest of the board, combined, gives $10,000, and each member contributes.

Create a Fundraising Competition between Board Members

Challenge board members to come up with a new, creative way to challenge themselves. Give them some examples that have worked in the past. I have coached organizations where we decided to set an overall board goal, for example, $25,000. One board member was able to give $10,000. Another was able to give $3,000 and seven gave $1,000 each. The remaining board members each gave gifts of $500 or smaller, and in total the board gave a gift of $25,000. The challenge was to get the board giving to that number and without the challenge, the $10,000 donor might not have stepped up.

Another way to create competition is to have a generous board member call the others and let them know what the board member is giving, and ask others to match it or give what they can.

The fact is that board members must give and get to help jump-start your fundraising this year. Once the entire board has given, you can "check off" one of your fifty asks.

Getting Your Board Involved in Fundraising

The "Get" of Give and Get

Board members should help the organizations they serve with all four stages of fundraising: identification, cultivation, solicitation and stewardship. As discussed in Chapter One, most board members say they do not want to fundraise, but what they really mean is that they do not want to ask (or solicit). In the following sections, I will discuss different ways to involve board members in each of the stages of fundraising.

Motivating Board Members to Identify

One of the biggest ways that board members can help nonprofits with fundraising is by "opening doors," or introducing others to the organization. In other words, board members can utilize their personal and professional rolodexes to introduce their friends, family and colleagues to the executive director, other staff and board members, and introduce them to the organization. This includes scheduling meetings and bringing friends and family to events and organization functions.

Board Members and Cultivation

Board members should arrange for meetings for the executive director with people who might be interested in the mission of the organization and who have some capacity to make a gift. Ideally board members will attend these meetings, whether they are at a home, office, restaurant, or at the organization's offices. If appropriate, a tour of your organization's facility can be a great first meeting with a prospect. If the board member is unable or unwilling to attend the first meeting, it is enough for the member to make the connection or introduction between the prospect and someone at the organization so that a meeting does take place.

There are many types of cultivation activities and depending on the prospect and the size of the prospective donation, this stage can take place over months or years.

Some great ways for board members to participate in cultivation include:

◆ Host a house party. A house party is at the home of a board member or other friend of the organization. The host often covers the cost of food and drink, so the expense to the organization is minimal. These cultivation events are opportunities for the executive director and board members to meet prospects in an informal setting. Generally there is a brief presentation about the organization with an opportunity for questions and answers. I recommend planting some questions with board members in the audience to get the conversation going.

After an initial introduction of the prospect to the organization at the house party, it is the responsibility of the development staff or executive director to follow up and schedule one-on-one meetings with attendees to gage their level of interest and get them involved with the organization.

◆ Give a tour. Board members can volunteer to go on or lead tours of the organization's facilities to their friends, family members and colleagues.

◆ Schedule a meeting. Arranging for a meeting between the executive director and prospect is a great cultivation tool. As stated above, the meeting should take place at a location most comfortable and convenient for the prospect, such as in the prospect's home, office, or at a restaurant.

Board Members and Asking

Peer-to-peer solicitation is the best way to ask someone for a gift for your organization. An ask is often more heartfelt when coming from a volunteer who gives time and money, rather than from a paid staff

A few weeks back I was leading a board retreat where we discussed "give and get" in great detail. At the end of the retreat several of the board members went up to the executive director and handed her checks or made financial commitments for the year. Great! They got the message and stepped up to the challenge.

The same night, other board members asked to step off the board and be put in other volunteer positions with the organization. Also great! They also got the message that they needed to give and get. They were not prepared to make the commitment, so they stepped off the board, freeing up a space for someone else to join the board.

 stories from the real world

member. This is the reason that we want board members making asks. However, since we recognize and acknowledge how difficult this part of the process can be, we need to help them out as much as possible.

Give board members a variety of ways to get involved in asking. Let them choose the method that works best for them.

◆ Write a personal note on a solicitation (appeal) letter.

◆ Ask their company or another company they do business with to sponsor your event.

◆ Ask a colleague (friend or neighbor) with a foundation to consider a grant or gift to your organization.

◆ Make a face-to-face ask of someone they have been cultivating.

Thanking is Easy

Once a gift has been made to your organization, it is critical to thank the donor in many different ways. The rule of thumb is to thank a donor seven times before asking for another gift. This is a perfect opportunity for board members to get involved. Board members can steward donors in the following ways:

◆ Make thank-you calls.

◆ Write or sign thank-you letters.

◆ Say thank you in person.

◆ Send a thank-you e-mail.

◆ Say thank you publicly at an event or in a publication.

Each of these methods can be used by multiple people. For example, both a board member and a staff member can each send thank-you notes or make phone calls.

Educating Your Board on Fundraising

It is important that you do not expect that fundraising skills will come easily or naturally to your board members. They will all need continuing

◆ Create a job description for incoming or potential board members.

◆ Plan fundraising education throughout the year including at several regular board meetings and at a board retreat.

◆ Develop a formal orientation process for new board members.

◆ Start a thank-you calling program for board members to thank donors.

◆ Ask board members to add personal notes to all mail appeals.

education on the subject. In addition to an annual retreat, where at least a half day is devoted to fundraising, fundraising skills and expectations should be regularly integrated into board meetings. Do not expect board members who have a half-day training to suddenly rise to the challenge. They need support, reminders and encouragement. It is up to the executive director and development staff to help board members be successful in fundraising.

The executive director in the Stories from the Real World sidebar on page 35 had not wanted to hurt her board members' feelings by asking them to step off the board. The board members who stepped off had not wanted to offend anyone or admit to shirking their responsibilities by resigning from the board. By giving them the opportunity to step down, it helped everyone. By carefully explaining the roles and responsibilities that night, we gave them an easy out and all parties were happier and better off.

Activities to Engage Your Board

On a daily basis, your board members should be:

◆ Advocating for your organization by talking about it to friends, family, and colleagues.

On a monthly basis, your board members should be:

◆ Making thank-you calls to donors.

◆ Participating in cultivation activities such as sending newspaper articles, handwritten notes, e-mails or other correspondence to prospects.

On a yearly basis, your board members should be:

◆ Participating in cultivation activities such as hosting a house party for your organization.

◆ Personally inviting their contacts to your fundraisers.

◆ Soliciting prospects (making the ask) when appropriate.

To Recap

◆ Board members must make personal donations to your organization (give) and raise funds for your organization (get).

◆ Board members need training and ongoing education about their roles and responsibilities.

◆ Board members can help with all stages of the fundraising cycle.

Chapter Three

Making Bulk Solicitations Less Bulky

IN THIS CHAPTER

···➔ How to start a direct mail program

···➔ Electronic versus traditional mail

···➔ Personalizing and segmenting

···➔ About data and databases

C hapter Three is the first of the following chapters that addresses a specific fundraising category: bulk mail. I will use the term bulk solicitation and bulk mail interchangeably, and both terms include traditional and electronic bulk mail. You will learn why a strong bulk solicitation program is critical for a successful development program in the short and long term. I will review the importance of having a functional database, and what to do with it. At the end of the chapter, you should be able to implement several new techniques to increase the success of your bulk mail program.

The Importance of a Bulk Mail Program

If you do not already have a direct mail program—both traditional and electronic—I strongly encourage you to start one. Although direct mail is expensive, there are two important reasons to have a direct mail program. First, bulk mail is a wonderful way to raise unrestricted dollars. Second, your database will ultimately become your portal into the world of individual donors and major gifts.

Bulk solicitations/bulk mail/direct mail refer to traditional (snail mail) or electronic solicitations. **Bulk** means that multiple persons will be asked for a donation within the same solicitation (appeal letter, invitation or e-mail).

finition

---

What's in Your Database: Prospect Identification

I assume that you have a list of names and contact information for people who are interested in your organization, and hopefully that list is in an electronic database. A database is an electronic organization system for your list of names and addresses (data).

Regardless of the type of database you are currently using, your organization needs some type of electronic database to capture the names and contact information of your supporters and donors. If your organization (and list of supporters) is small (fewer than 1,000 or so names) you might be using Microsoft Access, which is fine. If your organization is using a fundraising software product, that is fine too, as long as you are capturing the basics, such as:

◆ First and last name and spouse's/partner's first and last name.

◆ Mailing address.

◆ E-mail address.

◆ Phone number (home, business, cell).

◆ Gift history with your organization—all donations, including ticket sales, etc.

Some examples of donor software are: Blackbaud's Raiser's Edge, DonorPerfect, eTapestry, and GiftWorks. There are many others as well. Each have pros and cons, but there is generally no need to buy the most expensive or complicated system.

If you do not already have a list or database of supporters, it is time to start one by identifying potential supporters of your organization. You can do this by collecting, from your board and staff members, names and contact information of people who might be interested in your organization. Each person should provide five to ten names to get your list started.

To build your list, collect information from the attendees of all of your events as well as contact information from all volunteers and donors.

The phrase "garbage in, garbage out" is important to remember and refers to keeping a clean list. Your list is only as good as the data in it. Be sure to have someone other than the person who is doing the data entry spot-check the list on a regular basis. This means that once or twice a month you (if you are not the one doing the data entry) should look up a few recent entries and make sure that they are being entered correctly.

Cultivation by Mail

The line between cultivation and solicitation can be blurry in a mass mailing. What I mean by this is that cultivation is generally an opportunity for the prospect to learn about the organization and for someone at the organization, usually the executive director, to learn about the prospect. However, the cultivation process in bulk solicitation is only one-way: the prospect learns about the organization, not vice versa. There could be a "soft ask" in a cultivation piece. (See Definition sidebar, next page, for the definition of soft ask.)

Newsletters (electronic or traditional) are great examples of a form of bulk cultivation. In other words, when you send out newsletters you are educating supporters and community members about your organization.

From a newsletter your audience should learn about your organization, upcoming events, success stories, volunteer opportunities, etc. Other forms of bulk cultivation include mass mailing annual reports, brochures, electronic newsletters, links to newspaper articles, and volunteer opportunities.

A **soft ask** is an indirect request for donations. For example, a soft ask could be a reply envelope included in a newsletter. The main point of the newsletter is cultivation and a way to provide information. It would not be a direct request for a donation, as an appeal letter would be.

definition

Newsletters are an important component of a comprehensive cultivation and marketing strategy.

Print (Traditional) Newsletters

Newsletters should have several components, including:

◆ Photos. Many people look at newsletters for the photos and never read a word. Photos should be clear, plentiful, and tell a story.

◆ Success stories.

◆ Organizational updates, including staff and programmatic changes.

◆ Fundraising, which should include some regular sections on giving such as asking for annual gifts, explaining planned gifts, or telling the story of a donor and the donor's gift to your organization.

Electronic Newsletters

Although your print newsletters can be sent electronically as PDF's, electronic newsletters are different from traditionally printed newsletters in that your target audience is often younger and more willing to engage and donate on-line. Online correspondence should be shorter than traditional newsletters. Ideally, it should be able to be viewed on a single screen with links to full stories. Always include a way to donate to your organization with a credit card via PayPal or other online giving service.

To Whom, How, and How Often Should You Mail?

I encourage organizations to mail (traditional) as frequently as they can. For counting your asks in this category, I am including any bulk mail that has a specific ask, including appeal letters, newsletters with business reply envelopes (BRE's) and invitations to events. An example of a year of mailings might include:

◆ One year-end appeal.

◆ Two newsletters (spring and fall).

◆ Two event invitations.

This would count as five mailings per year. If you can add one or two more, and then fill in your calendar with electronic mailings, you will be mailing approximately once a month.

The reason that traditional mail ("snail mail") is so important is that many people still enjoy receiving correspondence in their mailbox, and older people might not respond to electronic solicitations or newsletters. As more people become comfortable with donating online, it is more imperative that you provide both options to accommodate the most people possible.

Electronic mail is equally as important as traditional mail because it reaches a wide audience for a fraction of the cost. Once your organization is set up to send regular e-mail newsletters or e-blasts, this form of communication will enhance your traditional mail program. Electronic communications should be interspersed with traditional mail throughout the year.

I recommend mailing to people frequently because studies have found that donors are more likely to give again the more recently they have given. Let me explain: If you have a donor who gives to you annually but skips a year, that donor is less likely to give in subsequent years. It makes sense that "lapsed" donors would be harder to renew or "get back" than current donors. Similarly, those who have given to you in the last six months are more likely to give than those who have not given in a year. Yes, some people only give annually, but many will give more than once a year.

Lapsed donors are donors who have stopped giving or former donors. This is generally measured by a year, and someone is considered lapsed if they have not given in the last twelve months.

I know that I am guilty of letting envelopes stack up in a pile from organizations to which I intend to give. Sometimes it takes them mailing me two or even three envelopes before I actually sit down and write a check.

If your organization does not currently have a mail program, the people on your list will need to get accustomed to the idea of being asked and giving to your organization through traditional mail or Internet (if they are not already doing so). When planning your direct mail strategy for the year, intersperse your traditional direct mail program with electronic mail messages.

Once a system is established and e-mail addresses are collected, sending e-mails to your list should be a relatively easy and inexpensive process. E-mail is a great way to keep in touch with donors and prospects and keep them updated about your program. For example, whenever your organization appears in the news, send an e-mail with a link to the news site.

However, people are inundated with e-mail these days, so make sure to keep your e-blasts short and valuable. It should include upcoming volunteer or other opportunities with your organization in addition to always including a link for giving.

There is no excuse for organizations that do not accept donations via credit card these days, because so many donors are giving with credit cards online. PayPal is one service that is a fast, easy and inexpensive way to accept credit cards online.

E-Mail, Social Media and More

If your organization does not have an up-to-date, interactive website, then it is seriously behind the times. Savvy donors are researching organizations before making donations and the place they start their search is online and at your website. If you do not have a comprehensive website, the donor might not have confidence in your organization. In addition to accepting donations, your website should allow visitors to sign up for your mailing list and volunteer opportunities.

While the jury is still out with regard to the comparative success of electronic fundraising versus traditional mail, we are seeing more and more examples of hugely successful online campaigns every day. The Red Cross and disaster relief efforts immediately come to mind with regard to successful online campaigns. However, there are also smaller organizations achieving successes in these areas. Even if Internet fundraising is not a major component of your campaign plan, it should be there and expanded on each year.

All correspondence should tell recipients how they can donate to your organization. Traditional mail should include a Business Reply Envelope (BRE) and e-mail should contain a link to accept credit card information as well as information about where to send checks.

practical tip

It is also important to be visible on social networking sites such as Facebook and LinkedIn. If you or someone in your office does not have the ability or time to maintain and monitor these sites, a great low-cost option is to consider hiring a college student to help you keep up with the trends and times.

Writing the Solicitation

Correspondence, whether traditional or electronic, should tell a story. Use quotes and photos, and explain how donations are being used. To be considered a solicitation as part of your fifty asks, a mailing must also directly ask for a gift and provide an easy method to return a gift to the organization.

Appeal letters should be mailed multiple times per year, but at minimum once a year in October/November, in time for year-end giving. Letters should be well written, with no grammatical errors or typos. The letter or solicitation should carefully explain your case for support as well as tell a story of how the organization has fulfilled its mission over the last year. Individual or personal stories are generally the most effective. Use quotations from clients and photos when appropriate.

Bulk solicitations are so important because they are the way that most individuals begin giving to an organization. It is through direct mail that supporters of your organization can identify themselves to you as interested in the mission. People who give through direct mail reveal themselves to you as individuals who care about your cause, and are therefore potential prospects for increased annual giving and possibly major gifts.

Getting Gifts

If you expect to receive donations through bulk solicitation, you have to ask for them and provide an easy way for people to give. Always provide a BRE in traditional mail solicitations and a link to a donation page in e-solicitations. The link should be to a secure page that accepts credit card information. If your organization does not accept credit cards, consider creating an account with PayPal which is an easy and inexpensive way to begin accepting credit cards.

If you are creating your first BRE or reply card insert, collect others from several organizations and use the components of those you like best. Remember to check with your bookkeeper and data entry staff member

◆ Appeal letters should ALWAYS include a business reply envelope (BRE) so donors can easily send in their donations.

◆ Whenever possible, letters should be personalized—addressed to the recipient, not "Dear Friend."

◆ Have board members, staff and volunteers take the time to write personal notes on as many letters as possible and certainly to all past donors. The more personal the letter can be, the better.

◆ First class (live) stamps on outgoing letters are highly recommended to make the mailing look less like bulk mail. However it is NOT necessary to put stamps on BRE's. That being said, if you can segment your list and add first class stamps to BRE's going to your highest donors it will help return rates, and is well worth the extra expense.

◆ Give donors the option to pay in monthly installments. If you do not have the capacity to take credit cards or automated payments, I would not recommend this type of program beyond board members because it will be too difficult to administer and collect payments. However, if you have an automated system, this is a great way for a $10 donor to become a $120 donor. This works well on all levels, by turning $1,000 donors into $4,000 donors with quarterly payments, etc.

◆ Ask returning donors for larger gifts by including specific ask amounts in your letter.

One of the main goals of bulk mail is to have it get opened before going in the trash. If your letter looks too much like bulk mail, recipients are likely to throw it away before opening it. The more an envelope appears to contain personal mail, the more likely a person is to open it and therefore read it.

Recently I received an appeal in the mail. The reply card had space for how much I wanted to give and for credit card information. However, nowhere on the card was space for my name, address or any other contact information! I cannot imagine what the charity did after receiving a credit card donation from someone, but not knowing who it was! I am sure this was an oversight, but it was a huge mistake.

 **stories from the real world**

to review the data requested on your BRE to make sure you are capturing what they need and in a format that makes sense. More sets of eyes are always better than one when reviewing something before printing and mailing. Appeals are a fantastic opportunity to enhance your database by collecting e-mail addresses, phone numbers, address updates, and other personal information about your donors.

Unlike appeal letters, newsletters are an indirect way of asking for contributions. In order to be considered an ask for counting asks, a BRE must be included or link for online giving. If there is no formal ask (BRE or link) then a newsletter should be considered a marketing piece or cultivation, but not counted as a solicitation.

Thanking the masses (en bulk)

Although this might seem obvious it does not always happen, so I am going to say it: Before sending your bulk solicitation, have the thank-you letters written and prepared to go out.

Industry standard is that thank-you letters should be turned around (mailed out) within 48 hours of an organization receiving a gift. In practice, I only know of a few organizations that actually get them out that fast. If you wait until donations start arriving to write the letter and you need to wait to get approval from the executive director, then it is going to take much longer to get the letters out the door.

Before sending the request (appeal) in the first place, have your stewardship plan and process in place.

◆ Know who is responsible for generating and sending the thank-you letters.

◆ If possible, have different letters for different donors—first-time donors, repeat donors, high donors (and know at what level they get the different letter), board members, etc. Each letter will be similar and might only have a few words or sentences that distinguish it from the other letters.

◆ Know which letters should be hand signed. Determine what the criteria are for getting a hand signature and/or personal note. Certain gift level? Board member? Etc.

◆ Arrange for thank-you calls to be made to certain donors. Know at what levels donors will be called.

◆ Know how gifts will be acknowledged in other ways, such as by multiple people, by e-mail, by phone, in public, newsletter, at an event, etc.

◆ Know what you will do after a letter has been sitting on the signer's desk (often the executive director's) for three days, one week, two weeks.

It is important to have your stewardship plan in place prior to sending the solicitation so you can get the process started as quickly as possible once the gifts start coming in.

Tracking Success

There are many ways to track the success of your bulk solicitations. In order to keep track, add codes to BRE's ("Fall Appeal 2010" could be "Fall-10") or code responses within your database. The codes will let you know which gift came from which appeal.

Track the number of people you mailed to with each solicitation, how many responded, the total amount given, the average gift size for that solicitation, and the high and low gift amounts.

Compare each appeal with the same appeal over subsequent years to know if your donations are increasing or decreasing. Track the number of returning donors, lapsed donors, LYBUNTS (Last Year But Not This Year) and SYBUNTS (Some Year But Not This Year).

Use the tables provided to count the number of times per year you plan to be in touch with your supporters through traditional and electronic bulk mail. Sending a bulk solicitation once a month is a great goal. Intersperse appeals, newsletters, invitations, and electronic mail evenly throughout the year.

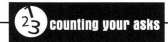

Use this chart to track and compare the success of your appeals. You will want to create a similar chart, tracking the same appeal (winter appeal, for example) over multiple years.

Solicitation Name/Date Mailed	Number Mailed	Number Donations	Total Gifts	Average Gift	High/Low
Example	*2,000*	*180*	*$11,000*	*$61*	*$900/$10*
Update E-mail Feb 2010					
Spring Appeal March 2010					
Spring Newsletter April 2010					
Gala Invitation May 2010					
Electronic Mini-Newsletter June 2010					

Bulk Solicitation Calendar

Create a calendar for your bulk asks, including invitations, appeals, newsletters, and e-mails so that you are sending to prospects on a regular basis. Each month should have one scheduled contact with prospects, donors and friends. Fill in the grid with the name of each solicitation and mail dates for each month.

Month	Appeal Newsletter	Invitation	Email
Example	Spring Appeal March 5	Gala Invite March 30	
January			
February			
March			
April			
May			
June			
July			
August			
September			
October			
November			
December			

To Recap

◆ If you do not have a bulk solicitation program, you need to start one.

◆ If you do not keep track of contact information of donors and supporters in a database, you need to start.

◆ Mail and e-mail as frequently as possible to keep in touch with donors and prospects.

◆ It does not matter how good your solicitation is if it does not get opened.

◆ Personalize, personalize, personalize.

◆ Board members can help with bulk solicitations in many ways including sending solicitations to their contacts, adding personal notes to solicitations, making thank-you calls, and more.

◆ Have a stewardship strategy prepared prior to mailing.

◆ Track your success.

Chapter Four

Incorporating Individuals into Your Development Plan

IN THIS CHAPTER

···→ The importance of including individuals in your development plan

···→ How to start an individual-giving program

···→ Identifying, cultivating, soliciting, and stewarding individuals

C hapter Four is one of the most important chapters because individual solicitation is the weakest area of development for most small and mid-sized nonprofits. I will review in detail the four stages of fundraising with regard to individuals, including how to identify prospects, detailed cultivation strategies, specific solicitation techniques, and ideas for stewardship. At the end of this chapter you should fully understand the importance of incorporating an individual-giving program into your development plan, as well as have the tools to implement it.

Why You Need an Individual-Giving Program

According to Giving USA 2010, individuals give 75 percent of the charitable dollars given to nonprofits each year. That number rises to over 80 percent when bequests are included, which leaves corporations and foundations contributing less than 20 percent.

If your organization is like most small nonprofits, your fundraising efforts are heavily focused on corporations and foundations and not nearly enough on individuals. Do you know what percentage of your organization's income is from individuals? What percentage comes from foundations and corporations? And what percentage comes from government?

There are a variety of reasons why organizations concentrate their fundraising efforts on corporations and foundations, and not on individuals. One of the major reasons is that fundraising from individuals is complicated and time consuming. Corporations and foundations appear to be easier to fundraise from because of their written and less-personal guidelines, making the process more understandable and clear cut. However, if you want your organization to raise big bucks and you are not already soliciting individuals, you will need to dive into this unknown territory.

Many organizations do not fundraise from individuals because they don't know where to start. If you can relate, read on.

Identifying Prospects—Whom to Solicit

When trying to figure out for the first time who your individual prospects are, your database can be a goldmine. If you have a database of any type (as discussed in Chapter Three, it does not have to be an expensive fundraising database) you should be able to extract your donors and identify prospects.

It is also important to have a staff member or volunteer who can obtain relevant information (reports) from your database as well. For example, when trying to identify prospects for your organization, the first two things to look for in your data are your highest and most loyal donors. You will need to run reports in your database to find these people.

Your highest donors

High donors can be defined in many ways, so look for all of them to be sure you have appropriately captured everyone you intend to. Run reports to list the largest single gifts given in a particular year (generally the most recent one or the last eighteen months), cumulative total giving for that year, and lifetime-high giving. Looking for cumulative giving in a year is important because you might have one donor who gives $1,000 per year in December and another who gives $100 monthly. The second donor will not come up in your top donors list if you do not total the gifts. However, that donor is clearly a larger donor than the first. Remember to include event income.

Your most loyal donors

When looking through your database for your organization's most loyal supporters you want to look for the people who have consistently supported the organization over a long period of time, regardless of their giving level. If you have the data, look back for those individuals who have given every year for five, ten or more years even if it is only twenty-five dollars (or less) per year. If they have the capacity, these are your most likely candidates for planned gifts (and major gifts) as they are your most loyal donors.

There are a few additional important points about loyal donors:

Acquisition refers to the number of new donors you have each year. For example, if an organization acquires 100 new donors per year out of 1,000 total donors, 10 percent of its donor base is comprised of acquisitions.

Retention refers to the number of donors you are able to keep from year to year. What percentage and number of donors are you keeping (or retaining)?

It is much easier and less expensive to retain donors than it is to acquire them, which is why cultivation and stewardship are so important!

◆ Donor acquisition and retention is a major issue for most nonprofits. Therefore, you should know who your loyal supporters are and treat them as VIP's.

◆ If you do not already know these people, you should find out who they are, why they are so loyal, and if they are interested in getting more involved with the organization. If they give a little without any attention, they might give significantly more with some cultivation and involvement.

For those organizations that do not have data or databases to rely on, you will need to create a list from scratch to start with. Refer back to Chapter Three about working with your staff and board to create your first list of supporters.

The individuals you include on your prospect list should have inclination **and** capacity.

Inclination means that individuals are philanthropically minded, and have an interest in your organization or cause.

Capacity means that individuals have the means (or ability) to make a gift.

Once you have lists of donors, select the top twenty to thirty individuals that you think have capacity and inclination. Do not choose these names in a vacuum. Ask staff and board members if they know the people on your lists, then make educated decisions about who to keep on your final, first-year prospect list. If you have a lot of names on your list, it is a great opportunity to become acquainted with your largest donors. Keep this longer list of names and use it for cultivation activities such as house parties, volunteer activities, event invitation lists, etc.

After you have narrowed your lists to the top twenty to thirty names, you should have a goal of actually cultivating and soliciting approximately ten to fifteen of those people this year. Start with a longer list because several people on the list will not have both capacity and inclination. Starting with a larger list ensures that you will have people left after eliminating those who cannot or will not be cultivated or solicited.

Individual Prospects

List your individual prospects for the year. Post this list above your desk and review it daily. Treat these individuals as VIP's for every cultivation and solicitation you do.

	Name	Contact Info Phone/Email	Relationship to Organization	Ask Amount	Ask Date
Ex.	Ms. Smith	(123) 456-7890 smith@aol.com	Friend of Board President	$2,500	June
1.					
2.					
3.					
4.					
5.					
6.					
7.					
8.					
9.					
10					
11.					
12.					
13.					
14.					

Cultivation—Relationship Building

Cultivation can take many forms and is an ongoing process, but it is ultimately about building relationships between prospective donors and individuals (executive director and board members) at the organization. Cultivation involves routine and regular contact with individual prospects, and is about educating them about the organization and getting to know them. Building relationships in this context means learning what these individuals are passionate about and gaining an understanding of what motivates them to give.

One of the most common mistakes made by executive directors, development directors and board members is that they are so eager to tell the story of the organization that they forget to listen. Listening to and hearing the person you are cultivating is an important part of the process that fundraisers often miss.

Cultivation plans should include any combination of the following:

◆ Regular visits to the home or office of the individual.

◆ Tour of the organization or program.

◆ Invitations to the organization's fundraising and programmatic events.

◆ Communicating information about the organization via regular calls, e-mails and written correspondence.

◆ Updates on program progress and successes—and setbacks.

◆ Invitations to volunteer in a variety of capacities.

In the cultivation stage, the cultivator must get to know the prospect and educate the prospect about the organization. During cultivation, it is your opportunity to involve the prospect in a meaningful volunteer capacity.

Each person on your list should have an individualized cultivation plan. (See the sample plan on page 67.)

Prospects can be divided into two major categories: those you already know and those you do not. The people you know should be easier to get meetings with or get involved in your organization because they are often already familiar with you or your organization.

The trickier part is developing relationships with individuals you do not know. Often it is helpful and necessary for a board member to make an introduction if the board member has a relationship with the person. A board member can introduce someone to the organization by:

◆ Calling to ask the individual to meet with the executive director.

◆ Inviting the individual to take a tour of the organization's facilities.

◆ Inviting the individual to an event, either as a guest or as a sponsor/ticket buyer.

◆ Inviting the prospect to a house party at the home of a board member or other volunteer.

There might be some people on your list who no one knows—people you found from your data search. Although it might be harder to get your foot in the door, the individual is already a donor to your organization so that the person should be receptive to contact from you. To make contact with someone new:

1. Send a letter of introduction to the individual. First, thank the person for supporting the organization, and second, state that you are interested in meeting and will be calling within a week.

2. Follow up on your letter within the designated time frame by phoning. If you get a machine, leave a message. Most phones have caller ID these days and if you hang up, they will know you called anyway.

3. When you reach the donor, express appreciation for past support and indicate that you would like to say "thank you" in person. Tell the donor that you would also like to learn more about what the

person loves about your organization. You can also update the person about the program during the visit. You can honestly say that you will NOT ask the person for money on this visit. (Remember, this is the cultivation stage, not the solicitation stage.) Do not say that you will NEVER ask for money, but that you will not ask on this visit. This is a visit for you to get to know one another.

Who should meet with the prospect?

Ideally a first meeting should include someone the prospect knows, such as a member of your board or the executive director. First meetings will often include two people from your organization such as the executive director and a board member or development director. However, even if no one on your board or staff knows the prospect, the meeting should take place between the prospect and the executive director and board member, if available and appropriate. When the executive director is unable or unwilling to meet with prospects, then the development director can initiate and attend the meeting.

Where should you meet a prospect?

Over the course of building a relationship, you will most likely meet with a prospect on many occasions and the meetings will take place in a variety of locations. Meetings can take place at your organization's premises, at the individual's home or office, or at restaurants. The first meeting should take place wherever the prospect is most comfortable, such as at their home or office. A common misconception is that prospects should be taken out for a meal. Restaurants are often noisy and can be awkward for a first meeting. Other complications over meeting at a restaurant include where to go, how to talk and eat at the same time, who pays, etc. All of these issues can be avoided by meeting at a home or office.

What is the goal or outcome of the first meeting?

The goal of a first meeting with a prospect is to learn more about the individual: why the person is interested in the organization, what motivated the person to give (if already a donor) and if the individual is interested in being more involved in any way. Another goal is to answer any questions the prospect might have about the organization and to give an overview/summary of the good work you are doing, including any relevant success stories. Be careful not to do all of the talking. This is a unique opportunity to learn about the prospect and get the person more involved. Ask open-ended questions including:

◆ *What motivates you to give to this organization? For example, is there a history of cancer in your family? Why do you feel it is important to have a clean environment? What was it about your education here that impacted your life?*

◆ *Are you interested in being more involved with our organization, and in what capacity? Can I tell you more about some of the ways to become involved?*

◆ *Which of our programs is most interesting to you and why?*

You should never leave any meeting without a follow-up plan or next steps. Next steps can include things such as a next meeting date to follow up, a promise to send materials or information, or providing additional information by phone.

A true cultivation process (relationship building) might take many months or even years before getting to the solicitation stage. This will depend in each case on the size of the gift you are seeking and the individual.

Solicitation—The Ask

When board members and executive directors say they do not want to fundraise, they are generally talking about the "ask" or solicitation. They do not understand that fundraising is a process, and often think of it as making cold calls or begging for money. Other reasons that people do not want to fundraise include fear of rejection, and discomfort or embarrassment of asking friends for money.

As I have discussed, fundraising is a long process. In reality the "ask" is actually only a single moment in time and only takes a moment, whereas

At a solicitation meeting it is important that once the ask has been made, the asker(s) be quiet. The next person to speak must be the prospect. This is because if you speak before the person has a chance to respond, you are likely to backpedal. You might take silence to mean something it is not (the prospect might just be thinking) and you might say something like "it's okay to say no" or ask for less even before the prospect says anything.

Remember, after the ask is made, be quiet. The prospect needs to be the next one to speak no matter how long or awkward the silence.

practical tip

the other stages of fundraising could take months or even years.

Prior to going to ask someone for a gift, you should prepare by role playing with the other people who will be attending the meeting. Each person at the meeting should have a specific role. For example, first, the board member would thank the person for taking the time to meet and for the person's past support. Next, the executive director would remind the person of the impact that prior support has had on the program and discuss the progress that has been made this year. The executive director could also talk about the upcoming projects and what they hope to accomplish. Finally, the board member could wrap up the meeting by asking for the gift—for a specific amount.

Regardless of the agreed-upon roles, someone must be responsible for making the ask. However, as a staff member you must be prepared to make the ask if the board member freezes during the meeting (which has been known to happen). Do not leave the meeting until the ask has been made. Have a transition phrase in mind to help you get to the ask if the end of the meeting is approaching and the ask has not yet been made.

There are many reasons that people say "no" when they are asked for a gift. If you are truly listening during the cultivation process, you should be asking good questions and learning the answers to these important issues prior to making an ask. The reasons that people say "no" include:

◆ I was asked by the wrong person.

◆ I was asked for the wrong project.

◆ I was asked at the wrong time.

◆ I was asked for the wrong amount.

◆ I am not committed enough to this organization.

Most of these issues could be avoided if the solicitor had only done a better job of listening during the cultivation process and learned the answers to many of these important questions.

Be prepared for these responses and ask open ended questions to learn more. For example, if the person says "I need to think about it" or "not now," ask questions to help understand what they are thinking and so you will know how to proceed.

Who is the right person to ask?

Ideally the best person to do the ask is a board member who knows the prospect, is a peer with the prospect and has been involved in the cultivation process. If a board member is unable or unwilling to do the asking, the member should at least be present during the meeting. If not a board member, the ask often falls to the executive director, and short of that it falls to the development director.

Although there is a better way and a worse way of asking, I have seen too many organizations that, "trying to get it right," never get around to asking. Unfortunately, in that scenario the ask never gets made. It is better that the development director make the ask than no ask get made at all.

How much should you ask for?

This is one of the most difficult questions to answer. In large development shops with dedicated prospect research staff, it is often possible to find out a great deal about an individual's assets and wealth. In a small shop, however, a quick Google search and a discussion with staff or board members who know the prospect will generally suffice.

Determining the amount also depends on what you are looking for. Are you requesting an annual gift (yearly) or a capital gift (for a special one-time project)?

Determining how much to ask for will depend in part on a variety of factors that must be taken into consideration, including:

◆ What is the giving history of the individual to your organization and others?

◆ Without too much research, what do you know about the person's lifestyle and assets? What type of job does the person and spouse or partner have? Do they have children to support and/or college tuition to pay? How many vacation homes or what type of vacations do they take?

◆ What are other board members/peers saying about them and their spending and earning?

During the cultivation process it is up to you to try to determine what level of gift might be achievable. You can do this by giving examples of things you need. For example, ask if the person would be interested in supporting a staff salary in the $100,000 range, or a week of program services for $10,000, etc. Once you have a figure in your head, ask for more!

When to ask?

You should ask for a gift as soon as you possibly can, once you feel that you know the answers to your cultivation questions and that you are confident that the person will say yes to your request. Do not drag the process out unnecessarily. I have heard too many stories of when an organization gets around to asking for a gift, the response is "I would have said yes, but another organization asked me last week."

Where to ask?

As discussed briefly in the cultivation section, it is often difficult to hold a productive meeting in a restaurant, and it is not a place to ask for a gift. You would not want to be asking for a gift in a restaurant only to have a waiter interrupt at exactly the wrong moment. Also, restaurants can be noisy and you want to make sure that everyone can hear the conversation and the ask!

The best place to ask for a gift is wherever the prospect feels most comfortable. This is often at the individual's home or office. This might seem uncomfortable for you at first, but if you have had several meetings there with the prospect during the cultivation stage, it should be natural and normal.

How to ask?

Perhaps asking for money is so difficult because we live in a society where talking about money is taboo. Here are some examples of ways to ask for money when you can't get the words out:

> ◆ Board member to prospect: "I hope you will join me and make a gift to this important organization in the range of $5,000 to support the programs we have discussed."

When asking a donor for a gift, use the term "in the range of" and then provide a single number. Don't actually give a range.

We use the term "range" when requesting a gift because it gives the person the opportunity to come back with a different amount rather than just a "yes" or "no" like asking for a specific amount would. However, we do not actually provide a "range" option, like $1,000 to $5,000, because the person would always pick the lower number.

◆ Executive director to prospect: "I hope you will consider a gift in the range of $5,000 to the afterschool program to be used for providing daily snacks for the children and a basketball clinic."

Soliciting gifts from individuals is a lot of work, but the end result is worth the effort. One major difference between fundraising from corporations and foundations versus fundraising from individuals is that individuals generally stay loyal to organizations throughout their lifetimes.

Corporations and foundations, on the other hand, can have personnel and policy/priority changes. New staff to corporations often come with their own interests and priorities and will select their own charities to give to.

Start with a list of twenty to thirty prospects and narrow it down for the first year to those who have capacity and inclination.

Include on your development plan a list of the ten to fifteen people you will solicit for a gift within the next year. Create a cultivation plan for each one.

Add the number of individuals you plan to solicit this year to your ask calendar.

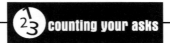

Stewardship—Follow Up

Stewardship is the "thank you" and follow-up stage of the fundraising cycle. After a gift is made, donors should be thanked frequently and in multiple ways, including:

◆ Formal receipt/letter with handwritten signature and note.

◆ Phone call.

Individual Cultivation/Solicitation Plan (Sample)

Personal Information

Name: _____

Contact Info: _____

Primary Contact (Board/Staff Mbr): _____

Secondary Contact: _____

Interest Areas (program names): _____

Giving History

Lifetime Giving Total: $_____

Highest Gift to Date: $_____

Average Annual Giving: $_____

Cultivation Calendar

	Meeting Date	Staff/Board	Location	Goal/Outcome	Next Step Follow Up
1					
2					
3					
4					
5					

Goal Ask Date: _____

Goal Ask Amount: $_____

◆ E-mail.

◆ In person.

A recent fundraising study showed that when donors were thanked by a board member (via phone) within forty-eight hours of making a gift, their subsequent giving increased by over 37 percent! A great way to involve your board members in the fundraising process is to ask them to be involved in thanking donors.

It is important to be prepared with your stewardship strategy before launching a campaign of any sort (annual, capital, event, etc.) whenever a large number of gifts are expected.

Stewardship often gets less time and attention than other stages of the fundraising cycle, but this crucial stage helps with donor retention and increased future gifts. Remember to integrate this important stage into your fundraising plans and processes.

Major Gifts: How Big is Major?

While this is certainly not a book on major gifts, I thought it would be negligent of me to not mention them. Unfortunately, I think there is much confusion as to what they are, and how they are requested and received. I have heard many board members say that they want to hire a development director to "go out and get major gifts." I always want to ask them, *go out where and ask whom?*

Fundraising is not magic and development staff members are not magicians, much to the great disappointment of many board members I have worked with. Fundraising success takes the time and effort of a team of people who are passionate about a cause and a willingness to build relationships based on that passion.

To me, the term "major gift" means different things to different organizations. For larger institutions such as universities and hospitals, a major gift might start at $100,000 or more. For smaller organizations, a gift of $10,000 or even $5,000 might be major.

The term "major gift" could also apply to individuals. A major gift for one person might not be a major gift for someone else. For example, one donor will consider $2,000 to be a major gift, while another can give ten times that amount and even then it is not a significant amount for the donor.

It is important to understand that if you are just beginning an individual-fundraising program, it is unlikely that you will be receiving any "major gifts" in the near future. If you have never asked for or received major gifts before, practice asking for gifts for your annual fund from your best donors, before considering going out and asking for major gifts.

Start building a major gifts program by:

◆ Getting to know your donors on an individual basis and making them "friends" of your organization.

◆ Providing meaningful volunteer opportunities.

◆ Generating a list of needs with corresponding dollar amounts ($1,000 +) for your annual fund.

◆ Asking for gifts for your annual fund.

◆ Stewarding those donors and begin cultivating them for major gifts.

Once you have successfully cultivated and solicited gifts from individuals for your annual fund, you will be able to start cultivating those same donors or others for major gifts.

Planned Giving—Testamentary Gifts and Beyond

A planned gift is a donation to a charity that involves tax, income and other benefits to the donor and/or donor's family beyond the basic charitable deduction. These gifts also require "planning" on the part of the donor and often involve their accountants and/or attorneys. Examples of planned gifts include testamentary gifts (gifts at death that can be made by will or trust), annuities, life insurance, charitable trusts and real estate.

If you are starting a planned giving program from scratch, the first step is to determine what type of gifts your organization can easily and practically accept. For example, a gift of fine art or property could cost more to maintain and sell then you actually receive from the sale. These gifts are generally not productive to accept when you are just starting out. Your organization might want to ask the donor to sell the item and donate the proceeds (which the donor might or might not agree to do) rather than accepting the item. You might need to have a policy to not accept this type of gift.

Once you have determined the types of gifts you can and are willing to accept, publicize it. Create a section in your newsletter and on your website letting people know that you now accept certain types of gifts, and list them. If nothing else, you can certainly accept testamentary gifts and current gifts of stock. Connect with an estate attorney through your board to provide language about testamentary gifts to have on your website and in your newsletter. Ask current and former board members to be among the first to include your organization in their wills and trusts.

> Invite past and present board members to include your organization in their wills and living trusts to kick off your planned giving program. Once one has made a commitment, feature the person in your newsletter and on your website as an example to others.

to-do lists

When discussing an estate gift with a prospect, be sure to explain that when considering the inclusion of your organization in the person's will or trust, you know that family comes first. However, also explain that you hope that if your organization was important during the person's lifetime, a charitable gift at death could also be considered. Talk in percentages. Explain that while the person might want to leave 80 or 90 percent of the estate to heirs, something like 10 percent could be left to your organization and any other favorite charities. By giving them an example, the prospective donor will understand that the bulk of the estate can still go to family, while still supporting important causes.

Check out Leave a Legacy at www.leavealegacy.org to learn more about the basics of leaving an estate gift to charity.

To Recap

◆ Individual solicitation is a critical component of a solid development plan.

◆ The executive director is the visionary for the organization, and therefore the one to build relationships with top prospects.

◆ Board members can play important roles in each of the stages of fundraising, including helping identify prospects, opening doors for the executive director by setting up meetings and other cultivation events, writing notes on appeals and making asks for gifts, and finally, making thank-you calls and writing thank-you letters.

◆ It is important to have a solid annual individual-giving program before soliciting major gifts.

◆ Create cultivation plans for each individual prospect.

◆ Major gifts differ in size depending on the organization's capacity and access to major-gift prospects.

◆ Start a planned giving program by requesting testamentary gifts from board members and other supporters through personal requests and advertising them in your newsletter and on your website.

Chapter Five

Grant Research, Writing, and Relationships

IN THIS CHAPTER

- ┅➔ How to research grants and decide which are the best to apply to

- ┅➔ The importance of building relationships with foundation funders and how to get started when no prior relationship exists

- ┅➔ Writing grant proposals, attachments and budgets

G rant writing is probably the most popular form of fundraising for small nonprofits. Chapter Five will cover all aspects of writing and winning grants, from researching (identification) to stewardship. The importance of building solid relationships with foundation funders will be emphasized and broken down into steps. I will review how to determine which foundations to apply to, how much to ask for and when to apply.

If your organization gets more than 50 percent of its budget from grants, then feel free to skim through this section to make sure that your grant writing is as efficient and effective as it could be. But you should concentrate on other types of fundraising to ensure a balanced and diversified fundraising plan.

I am going to use the term "foundation" to refer to a wide variety of grant-making entities, including family, corporate, community and other foundations.

Government Grants—Pros and Cons

Government grants, whether federal, state or local are often highly competitive and challenging to complete. While they are an excellent source of funds for many nonprofits, they are not what we will be concentrating on here. Government grants can be for enormous sums of money and generally require huge amounts of reporting (sometimes not worth it for smaller nonprofits). I also believe that government funding will only continue to decrease as a resource, as it has done for many years, and is not a great place to look for funding if you are just starting out.

Research

How do you identify the foundations you will apply to each year? Are you active or passive when selecting foundations to apply to?

The obvious place to start is to reapply to those from which you received funding in the past. The challenge begins when it is time to identify new foundations. Many nonprofits select the foundations that they apply to in a "passive" way. By passive, I mean waiting for foundations to be brought to your attention. For example:

◆ You see a corporation presenting a check in the newspaper.

◆ You learn about an opportunity from a friend or colleague.

◆ You learn about a foundation that gives to your type of organization from an online discussion forum.

Organizations that identify potential foundation funders in this way do NOT actively research foundations, and do not even know what opportunities are available and that they might be missing.

As part of your fundraising plan, you should research foundations proactively and raise more money!

There are several good places to research grant opportunities, but the one I use is the Foundation Center which can be found at http://foundationcenter.org. Another popular site is Grant Station which can be found at http://www.grantstation.com.

When researching foundations, use key words to look for:

◆ Does the foundation provide support in the geographic area where the organization provides service? Some foundations will provide support to organizations regardless of where they are located, but most restrict their giving to one or two states, counties or even countries. In other words, a foundation may give in New York and New Jersey only or in several counties within one state, or an international foundation may give throughout the United States as well as in one or two additional countries.

◆ Do they fund the type of program that I am raising funds for? For example: Do they fund only children's programs or the environment or healthcare? Is my organization a good match?

◆ Do they provide the type of funding I am looking for? For example: unrestricted, program, salary, capital or endowment?

If you can answer "yes" to these questions, then you have a potential match. Do not ignore this fundamental information.

practical tip

The Foundation Center's database can be accessed for free from many physical locations nationwide. (Check its website for a current listing.) Call the site before going to make sure it really does have access and

---

After your research is complete, it is time to rank the foundations you have identified in order to decide which you will apply to this year:

A.   Perfect Match
"A's" are those foundations that are a perfect match in terms of your mission and that of the foundation. "A" foundations also give in your geographic area and provide the type of funding you are looking for.

B.   Good Match
"B's" are those where there is some overlap in mission and geography, but they also fund a wide variety of programs or locations. Or something else tells you that they are not a perfect match.

C.   Remote Match.
"C's" are those that upon first glance seemed to be a match, but with additional research turn out not to be a match after all. For example, as mentioned, if you find a foundation that funds children's programs, but you are looking for funding for a pre-school program and the foundation is interested in teenagers, then it is not really a good match after all.

Throw the C's in the trash. File the B's in the file drawer for a rainy day. If you have enough in the "A" category to last you the year, then you are finished with your active grant research and have probably identified several new potential sources of income. If you can handle more foundations than you have in the "A" pile, then you still need to do more research.

someone is available who can show you how to get on. You can also pay a fee to access the database from your desktop. However, before you do, I highly recommend spending a few hours at one of the free sites to do most of your research and determine if a paid subscription is right for your organization.

There is no need to spend all year researching and constantly adding foundations to your list. I advise my clients to do all their grant research in one day for the entire year. You can do this too.

In one day of research you can identify many foundations that could be great prospects for your organization that you did not know existed. Once you have taken this simple step, you have actively identified foundations to apply to instead of being passive about it.

Add the number of grants you plan to apply for to your total asks for the year.

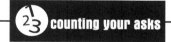

In order to find foundations that are good matches for your organization, make sure that you read and follow their guidelines and requirements exactly. If a foundation only funds organizations in New York and your organization is in Texas, do not waste your time (or theirs) applying. I know this seems obvious, but you would not believe the number of times applicants ignore this information.

Likewise, if you are looking for funding for a children's program, it is possible at first glance to think you found a match, but upon reviewing the foundation's website might find that it supports teenagers while your organization serves preschoolers.

After identifying as many prospective foundations as you can in a database of funders, continue your research by looking up each of the foundations' websites to get as much additional information as possible. Look for grant guidelines, deadlines, contact information, program priorities, etc. The Foundation Center, for example, only provides a snapshot of each foundation, so it is important to take this extra step. In order to get to fifty asks, your goal is to write at least one grant per month. You will need to determine how many re-applications plus new applications you can handle each year.

Before making your final selection of the grants you will write this year, review with your staff and board members lists of staff and board members at the foundations. If anyone at your organization knows

Grant Calendar

	Foundation Name	Application Deadline	Amount Requested	Contact Info	Notes
1.					
2.					
3.					
4.					
5.					
6.					
7.					
8.					
9.					
10					
11.					
12.					
13.					

someone at one of the foundations, this person can jump-start the relationship between your organization and the foundation.

Once you make your final list, if there are more in the "A" pile than you can handle in one year, you should sort them by how much they give. There is no sense in applying to smaller foundations that give $1,000 at a time, if you have more than enough to apply for that give in the $10,000 or more range.

Creating Your Grant Writing Schedule

After your research is complete and you have identified those to which you plan to apply, it is time to sort by due date. If most of the foundations you will apply to have specific due dates, then you can add them to your calendar. However, many foundations will accept applications year-round or have multiple deadlines (quarterly or semi-annually).

While many foundations accept applications year-round or multiple times of year, most foundations have "better" times of year to submit applications. For example at the "beginning" of the year (their fiscal year might or might not be January) some foundations give away much more in the first grant cycle than at the end of their year when they are running low on funds. If that is the case, as an applicant I would want to know the best time of year to apply to take advantage of the grant cycle that would give me the best chance for funding.

Also, most foundations that accept applications year-round probably have cut-off deadlines before board meetings that occur annually, semi-annually or quarterly. If you unknowingly miss a deadline, you could wait six months or more before your application is reviewed. On the other hand, if you find out the internal deadline schedule rather than just submitting it whenever you feel like, you might get an answer in six weeks. (We will discuss how to obtain this information in the next section. Keep reading.)

Once you know when you will apply to each foundation, add application deadlines to your grants calendar (see chart on page 78).

Building Relationships with Foundation Funders

At a grant-writing seminar I attended a few years ago, a program officer from a foundation said that most applicants never contacted him or his foundation except for submitting a grant application. After that, if the organization received funding, it submitted the required reports but nothing more. His point was that in most cases there is no effort made by the organization to build a relationship with the foundation. The speaker also said that he likes speaking to grantees and potential grantees, which is his job. Furthermore, he was puzzled about why more development officers and executive directors do not call him with questions. A program officer's job is to get to know nonprofits and support them. If you do not call, how can you build a relationship? Remember, fundraising is about relationship building.

Do you have relationships with your foundation funders?

Until that seminar several years back, I had been too intimidated to contact foundations. I had never called a foundation, because I never thought anyone would take my call. The speaker was so insistent that we call that I went back to the office the next day and picked up the phone. The results were remarkable! After calling three new foundations that month, I got new, first-time funding from each of the three. My results had never been that good before, but I was successful because I was able to refine my applications based on conversations with program officers at the foundations prior to submitting the applications.

The first time to call a foundation is before applying!

If you think your organization is a good match for a foundation, call and speak with a program officer to confirm that the program officer also thinks your program is a good match. You can also ask about application deadlines, if the foundation accepts applications year-round or has multiple deadlines. Prior to calling, come up with a list of thoughtful, thought provoking questions. For example:

◆ *I understand that you fund children's programs and our organization runs after-school programs. We are thinking of applying for tutors for three of our largest programs. Does that sound like it would be of interest?*

◆ *We have several programs that might be a good match for your foundation. Can you tell me which you think sounds like the best match?* (Then proceed to have quick descriptions of each program.)

◆ *Your website says you accept applications year-round. Is there a better time of year to apply? When does your board meet to review applications? Do you have a larger pot of money to give in the beginning of the year? When is the start of your fiscal year?*

◆ *Given the challenging economic circumstances, I was wondering if you are giving grants to new organizations this year?*

This is also a good time to ask when decisions will be made and when you might expect to hear about a decision. You could also invite the program officer to visit your organization for a tour. Offer to send the officer materials about your organization prior to submitting the application. Do not worry if the person says no because the program officer will remember that you are open to the idea.

After an initial conversation and if you decide to apply, the next time to call is one week after you mail your application to confirm that the foundation received it and to ask if there are any questions. Most program

1. Research foundations.
2. Rank your findings "A" "B" and "C."
3. Decide which you will apply to from your "A" pile based on how much they give and mission match.
4. Fill in your grant calendar.
5. Call foundations to build relationships and ask questions.
6. Apply for grants.

to-do lists

officers will not have questions at that time, but you are beginning to build a relationship with the foundation and you have planted a seed with the person about your organization as well as reintroduced yourself.

These before-and-after-the-application types of phone calls have proven to be highly productive for me. I am confident that they have raised the awareness of the program officer, who then took the time to thoroughly review my application. My first few calls are usually so positive that I would never consider not calling a foundation now.

That being said, not every foundation I call wants to have a lengthy conversation or any conversation at all. Many simply say they have not gotten to the applications yet and do not have any questions. However, by phoning I have educated them that I am diligent and my application stands out when they get to it.

After all your pre-application calls are complete, you can fill-in the due date on all of your applications and add them to your calendar.

I am frequently asked about foundations that do not advertise their phone numbers, or that proactively say they do not take calls. This generally occurs with small foundations (a family foundation without staff, for example) that do not have the capacity to answer calls. In these circumstances I try to find a connection to the foundation, such as one of

> Use social media to increase your chances of connecting with someone from a foundation. For example, use LinkedIn or Facebook to discover if anyone you know is acquainted with the person (or anyone else) who you are interested in contacting at a specific foundation.
>
> Do this by sending out a question on LinkedIn or Facebook to your contacts about the foundation or individual in question. You can also plug in the name of an individual into LinkedIn to see if you are connected in any way.

practical tip

my board members who knows one of its board members, to make an introduction. Social networking is great for these types of circumstances where you might be connected to someone on LinkedIn or Facebook to get an introduction through someone you know.

As in all fundraising, I believe your chances of receiving a grant will exponentially increase if you have a relationship with the funder. If a foundation decides not to fund your organization, you might be in a position to ask it if it could introduce you to other foundations that might be a better match.

Have someone outside of your organization review your grant application to make sure it makes sense to someone who is unfamiliar with your program. Also ask this person to check to make sure you have answered the questions as asked.

 practical tip

For foundations that do not have staff or that do not publish phone numbers, I have gone as far as looking up numbers of board members at their places of business. I have found that they generally take my call. And if they do not take my call, so what? I am no worse off than I was before I made the call.

Building relationships with foundation funders is the best way to ensure success in securing funds. It will also be critical to submit a solid and well-written application.

Writing Proposals

When preparing to write a grant application, first review and follow the application guidelines. I do not say this lightly, as I am aware of many otherwise good applications that got tossed in the trash for a technical error—not enough copies, a staple instead of a paperclip, single space instead of double, etc.

Some foundations have guidelines posted on their website and others will mail them to you. Many require an initial letter of inquiry before a full application.

Do not rely on a third party such as the Foundation Center for information, but get guidelines directly from the foundation itself whenever possible. Foundations often have much more extensive information on their own website or in their materials than what is listed at the Foundation Center or in other directories. If a foundation does not have a website, call to ask for grant guidelines.

I always use a hard copy of the guidelines and highlight, circle or underline the important items, including deadline(s), specific number-of-page requirements, spacing (double or single), binding requirements, font type and size, attachments, etc. After completing the grant application I refer back to my highlights to make sure I have done everything required before mailing it in. Most importantly, I stick to deadlines.

Applying for grants can be challenging, but if you have all the basic pieces of information written out in advance, a grant application is generally not more than a complicated cut-and-paste job. Each application needs to be tailored to the specifications of the funder, but in most cases you probably have a majority of the information and attachments on hand.

An important component of grant writing is remembering to answer the questions as they are asked. If you cut and paste a paragraph that you used from a different grant application, make sure it actually answers the question. Use examples, stories and statistics whenever possible and appropriate.

Finally, do not fabricate or exaggerate numbers of clients served or budget numbers, as foundations are familiar with what is generally possible for a given amount of funding. Even if you do get the funding with exaggerated numbers, it is unlikely that you will have the predicted results at the end of the year, and renewal funding will be especially difficult to get.

Attachments

There is some basic information that almost all foundations require. It is helpful to prepare multiple copies at once or have a file (paper and electronic) of highly requested materials that is readily accessible when you need it for future applications. This makes getting future applications "out the door" much easier and more efficient. The list includes, but is not limited to:

◆ Organization mission statement.

◆ Organization history.

◆ Project summary.

◆ Audited financial statements.

◆ 501(c)(3) IRS determination letter.

◆ Most recent annual report.

◆ Project budget.

◆ Organization budget.

◆ List of board members with affiliations.

Funding Request and Budgeting

How much should you ask for?

When trying to determine how much to ask for, I look at a foundation's previous year or two of giving, which can often be found on its website or in its annual report. If it gives in many programmatic areas, focus on the area in which you will be applying. I ask for an amount in the middle of its giving range, especially if the organization would be a first time grantee. I would never want to ask for the most, or, for that matter, the least, that it typically gives.

If last year it gave:

◆ 30 grants of $10,000,

◆ 100 grants of $25,000, and

◆ 3 grants of $100,000.

Foundation Cultivation/Stewardship Calendar. Insert date in each blank box.

Foundation Name	Send Thank You Letter	Report Deadlines	Invite on a Tour	Send Newsletter	Send Program Update Email	Send Gala Invitation	Reapplication Deadline
1							
2							
3							
4							
5							

TOTAL REQUESTED: $ _____

TOTAL RECEIVED: $ _____

I would ask for $25,000. In this example, $100,000 seems to be the exception to the rule and it seems extremely comfortable giving $25,000, so that is the amount I would apply for.

The amount you ask for also depends on how much your program costs. Very few funders want to be the sole supporter of a project. If your project budget is $30,000, you might try to target three foundations for $10,000 each.

Additionally, each foundation has its own rules about what they will and will not fund. If it allows a percentage of operating funding in addition to program items, you will want to ask for that. Many foundations will fund program salary line items. Knowing the answers to these questions in advance will help your budgeting process. Coordinate with the person who handles budgets in your office to come up with a project budget that works within the framework of your organizational budget.

Follow Up

Congratulations! You have been awarded the grant. Send a thank-you letter now! You might also want to call or e-mail the program officer you have started to build a relationship with to thank the person, especially if you are not the one signing the thank-you letter.

Create a calendar of cultivation and stewardship "events" for the year of how you will work to build your relationship with this foundation and others. For example:

◆ Send two newsletters per year (or as many as you produce) as well as your annual report and other publications.

◆ Send articles whenever your organization appears in the newspaper.

◆ Send e-blasts and regular updates.

◆ Invite program officers to visit your program two to three times per year, such as for a tour, fundraising events, client events such as graduations or programs, etc.

◆ Send all requested reports on time.

◆ Send or call in an update if there is a minor or significant change to the program or project it is funding, especially if there is a problem or delay with the project.

In the event that you do not receive the grant this time around, but you believe that the foundation is truly a good match for your organization, do cultivation activities anyway and apply again next year. Call the program officer to thank the foundation for considering your application and ask for any feedback as to why your application was not funded.

Building relationships will significantly increase your chances of getting the grant next time as well as ensure that you continue to receive funding into the future.

To Recap

◆ Actively research new grant opportunities each year.

◆ Increase your chances of receiving grants by building relationships with foundation funders.

◆ If you have more grant opportunities than you have time to apply for, prioritize those you have relationships with and those that give the most money per grant.

◆ Cultivate and steward your foundation funders like you would an individual donor.

◆ Keep attachments handy for ease of submission for future proposals.

◆ Submit grant proposals exactly as requested by the funder and be sure to answer questions as asked.

Chapter Six

Events Are Not About Ticket Sales. They're About Sponsorship!

IN THIS CHAPTER

···→ Making sure that events are as efficient and effective as possible

···→ Sponsorships are the key to generating lots of revenue from events

···→ Building a fundraising committee to help with your special events

···→ Follow up with VIP prospects who attend your events

C hapter Six will review the pros and cons of having events as well as what constitutes a successful fundraising event. I will discuss the basics of event planning, but focus even more on how to raise more money with your events. Many nonprofits have event committees that spend money, and I will explain the importance of having a focused fundraising committee. I will discuss how events have changed and how they have stayed the same in the new economy.

Events are Expensive

There are many pros and cons to having special events. One of the challenges of special events is that they are extremely labor intensive. Coordinating a well-planned special event requires many hours of work, generally by both staff and volunteers. Event fundraising is also the most expensive type of fundraising. So if events are so labor intensive and expensive, why do we have them?

The reasons we have events are:

◆ Events are unique occasions to showcase your organization to your current supporters and members of the community.

◆ Events are opportunities to raise a lot of money from companies and individuals that might not otherwise give to your organization.

◆ Events can be used as cultivation activities to engage prospects with your organization.

◆ The funds raised are unrestricted and can be used for operating expenses.

For these reasons, I am convinced that all nonprofits should have at least one fundraising event during the year. That being said, I strongly caution organizations that have many small fundraising events throughout the year because so many events are likely draining energy and resources of staff and volunteers.

One of the most common types of events among nonprofits is the awards dinner (or some variation). It serves as a friend-raiser and fundraiser. Fundraising events serve to:

◆ Raise funds.

◆ Build your database.

◆ Get your message out.

Sell Sponsorships, Not Tickets

Selling tickets is labor intensive. When I discuss tickets, I am talking about anything that you have to sell one at a time. The same holds true for cookie sales (except in the case of the Girl Scouts), magazine sales, card sales, bake sales, car washes, etc. These are bad fundraising events for any small organization because they are labor intensive and ultimately do not raise very much money. Schools might be the exception to this, but I do not consider them small organizations. They have huge labor pools (students) to do the legwork.

Due to the effort and expense required for most special events, I encourage small nonprofits (those that do not have a person dedicated to events) to host only one, or two at the most, fundraising events per year. If your organization has more than two events per year, you should carefully analyze each and consider which are truly making money after calculating staff time and expenses. Now is the time to cancel events that are not cost effective and are not providing a good return on investment.

Regardless of the economic climate, sponsorship (package pricing) is the way to raise significant amounts of money from event fundraising. The organizations I work with on events always have a ticket price for the individuals who will want to buy them, but the main fundraising focus should be on selling tables or sponsorship packages.

Events work the same way as any typical fundraising pyramid. This is where 20 percent of the donors give 80 percent of the dollars and 80 percent of the donors give 20 percent of the dollars. So start where 80 percent of the money is and try to get sponsorships.

Selecting a Committee

The purpose of an event committee is to help the organization raise money.

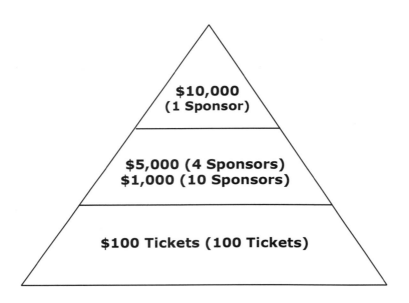

Sample Event Fundraising Pyramid

$10,000
(1 Sponsor)

$5,000 (4 Sponsors)
$1,000 (10 Sponsors)

$100 Tickets (100 Tickets)

Total Event Revenue: $50,000

115 Total Donors and Sponsors

Top 15 Donors (Sponsors) gave $40,000 or 80% of the dollars.

The remaining 100 donors gave $10,000 or 20% of the dollars.

If you have the right connections, it is almost the same amount of work to recruit a sponsor as it is to make a ticket sale.

On which should you spend your time?

I know this sounds obvious, but it is a novel concept to most organizations and I cannot emphasize it enough. Most event committees have members who spend money instead of raising it. They serve as an event planning committee and spend money on invitations, centerpieces, give-a-ways, music, food, and photographers. The list of event expenses goes on and on. Events should be planned by a staff member and one or two dedicated volunteers, but do not require committees of people to do the actual planning.

If your organization has a "money spending" committee, then it is time to "fire" the volunteers and start fresh. Yes, you can fire volunteers—in the nicest possible way of course. The executive director or development director should make a clear statement of what the fundraising goal for the event this year is, and request a commitment from each committee member to achieve that goal.

There is no better time than now to restructure your event committee. You can ask past committee members to commit to the new expectations or to step down, by honestly and carefully explaining that this year's event needs to be different. In order to succeed you will need a new kind of help from the volunteers serving on the committee. There will be some who stick around and rise to the challenge. Others will naturally, and quietly, slip away.

Some volunteers who are no longer appropriate for your new event committee should be asked to join other committees and stay involved in the organization in some other volunteer capacity. They are the volunteers who just do not want to or cannot help raise funds for the organization. In these cases, there are probably better committees for them to serve your organization. From now on call the event committee the "Event Fundraising Committee."

It will be much easier to plan the event if staff members make decisions like selecting vendors and menu choices, instead of having a committee discussion about it. However, you will want to keep volunteers who can generate in-kind donations and get you access to other resources such as free printing, alcohol or other goodies.

At least six to twelve months in advance of your event:

◆ Recruit a new fundraising committee for your event.

◆ Decide on the type of event you will have.

◆ Select a date and location.

◆ Set sponsorship levels.

◆ Recruit honorees and speakers.

◆ Solicit sponsors.

to-do lists

I understand that your organization might have one or two individuals who you will want to keep around who love their role as event planners. If these people are actually helpful because you are short staffed and they do help plan the event, fine. However most committee members just love to tell staff how to spend the money, but do not actually do any of the work. The other exception is if you have a volunteer who for "political" reasons you want to keep happy, such as your largest donor or the spouse of the CEO of a large company in town.

Now that you know real the purpose of the committee, it is time to form an event fundraising committee of board and non-board members. Ideally you should have people with recognizable names who probably will not do much work, but will raise money. You should also have some "worker bees" who are not recognizable on an invitation but who will also be able to bring in one or two sponsorships.

Let each committee member know up front that you expect them to buy or sell at least one table or sponsorship. If you have ten committee members, by the time you finish recruiting them, you will have already sold ten tables! Lay out additional expectations, such as attending two meetings, helping select and recruit honorees and speakers, etc.

At this point, or possibly many paragraphs ago, you might be thinking, *this author is out of her mind!* We will never be able to solicit people to serve on a committee like that. The good news is that committee members have additional important roles as well.

Committee member responsibilities, in addition to fundraising, include:

◆ Help select the type of event you will have.

◆ Help select and recruit speakers and honorees.

◆ Help set sponsorship levels and ticket prices.

It is important to have some key roles and responsibilities for committee members, in addition to fundraising, which will help make recruitment slightly easier as well as getting volunteers invested in your event. Committee members will select the type event you will have, with guidance from staff. If you have a room full of golfers, you could have a golf outing. Use committee resources and knowledge of the community to select an appropriate event for your community.

Committee members also have the privilege of selecting and recruiting speakers and honorees. Hopefully you have some committee members with access to people that you, as staff, would not ordinarily have access to—possibly a local celebrity, politician or head of corporation.

Finally, committee members set sponsorship and ticket levels, which I will discuss in detail in the "soliciting sponsors" section.

Planning, Timelines and Budgets

With the help of your committee, select the type of event you will have, a date and location. This should occur almost a year in advance of your event.

The most popular seasons for events are spring and fall. When selecting a date, try to find out when other fundraising events in your area will take place so there is no conflict. Once you select a date and time (which will depend on the type of event you choose to have), clear the final date with your committee, board members and honorees. Next on the to-do list is selecting honorees and speakers and getting the date on their calendars as well.

Before planning the event it is important to set a basic budget. Determine how much you will spend and how much you think you can raise, based on the number and level of sponsorships you expect.

Some expense budget items include:

◆ Venue

◆ Food

◆ Entertainment

◆ Decorations

◆ Invitations and Postage

◆ Ad Book/Program Journal

◆ Photographer/Videographer

◆ Audio/Visual

It is important to keep expenses as low as possible, especially in a down economy. Donors do not want charities to spend their dollars on a "party."

Selecting Honorees

Selecting honorees is a critical step to your fundraising success because the right honorees can buy and sell sponsorships for you as well as draw additional guests. Staff and volunteers should think of companies, individuals, foundations and groups that support your organization. Consider which of these companies, organizations and individuals

Basic Event Timeline:

Timeline	Task
1 Year Prior to Event	◆ Recruit committee ◆ Determine type of event ◆ Select date and book venue ◆ Select honorees and speakers ◆ Write budget
6-8 Months Out	◆ Determine sponsorship levels and benefits ◆ Set ticket prices ◆ Solicit key sponsors
4-6 Months Out	◆ Solicit all sponsors ◆ Reconfirm with speakers and honorees ◆ Design invitation and ad book ◆ Plan raffle, silent auction, etc.
2-4 Months Out	◆ Continue to solicit sponsors ◆ Order awards and plaques ◆ Get bios and photos from honorees ◆ Collect ads and logos for ad book ◆ Order and mail invitations
1 Month Out	◆ Send press release ◆ Finalize ad book ◆ Confirm with vendors (venue, music, etc.)
Week of Event	◆ Finalize numbers with venue ◆ Print nametags ◆ Make table assignments

(Chart continues on next page)

(Continued)

	◆ Assign staff and board roles
	◆ Match board greeters with donors/ prospects
Week After	◆ Send thank-you letters to all donors, honorees, and committee members
	◆ Make thank-you calls to all key volunteers and donors
	◆ Schedule follow-up with prospects

have the capacity and inclination to bring in funds. Always make this important decision as a committee with staff recommendations guiding the process. Select the best person to approach the honorees about being honored. Let honorees know what is expected of them up front, such as buying and selling sponsorships, providing a list of contacts to send invitations to, making a speech at the event, etc.

Soliciting Sponsors

Soliciting sponsors will be the most critical component of your event's success. As you will realize from the sidebar story, raising money through events is not about selling tickets, but about sponsorships.

Before you solicit sponsors, it is important to set sponsorship levels. As shown in the sidebar story, it is crucial to set them correctly. Setting sponsorship levels is an important role for the committee. Committee members are charged with buying and selling sponsorships, so they need to be able to do just that, which is why they set the levels.

Sponsorship levels can range from a bottom level of $500 to $50,000 or more, depending on the reach and capacity of your committee. Staff should make suggestions and guide the discussions, but committee members should be comfortable with at least the bottom level sponsorship amount, which they will need to buy or sell. Once a comfort zone is established, then three levels should be determined with the top level being a real stretch.

Companies and individuals expect to receive recognition and benefits in return for their sponsorship. You can create any recognition opportunities

Recently an organization hired me to help it with its annual fundraising event. I started by analyzing its sponsors and sponsorship levels from prior events. What I found was that the event had been raising approximately $50,000 annually (including $40,000 in sponsorship, plus ticket sales, silent auction, and journal ads). The top sponsorship opportunity was $5,000, and it had about eight sponsors at that top level. This immediately raised a red flag. If it could get eight sponsors at its top level, then its top level was clearly too low.

Although the staff and board resisted raising sponsorship levels, I convinced them to try a top level of $15,000, a middle level of $10,000, and a bottom level of $5,000. Even if they got no additional sponsorships, most of the old sponsors would still return at the $5,000 level.

As it turned out, the organization got three sponsors at the new top level ($15,000) for a total of $45,000, and two sponsors at the $10,000 level for an additional $20,000. From its first five donors (sponsors) it raised $65,000—more than it had ever raised at the event before. This was before it had sold a single ticket, journal ad, or silent-auction item. Needless to say, it went on to raise well over $100,000, more than twice what it had previously raised at the event.

you wish. This is an important opportunity to seek committee-member input to help determine what type of recognition they and their companies would want.

Here are some standard examples:

Friend Sponsor (Bronze):

- ◆ 1 table of 10

- ◆ Listing in the ad journal/program

- ◆ Table sign with your name

Supporter (Silver):

- ◆ 1 table of 10

- ◆ Half page in the ad journal/program

- ◆ Table sign with your name

- ◆ Recognition from the podium at the event

- ◆ Listing on our website for one year with link to your website

- ◆ Listing on invitation

Benefactor (Gold):

- ◆ 1 front row, premier table of 10

- ◆ Full page (or front or back inside cover) in ad journal/program

- ◆ Table sign with your name

- ◆ Recognition from the podium at the event

- ◆ Logo on our website for one year with link to your website

◆ Premier signage at the event

◆ Company logo on invitation

In order to generate the most sponsorship dollars for your event, you will need to begin soliciting sponsorships months before invitations go out. This is not something that is simply listed on the invitation. Separate sponsorship forms should be created and sent specifically to potential sponsors, along with pre-mailing phone calls and follow up calls or e-mails from a contact within your organization (often a committee member).

If you get one or two sponsors at the top level, the level should be high enough that you go screaming down the halls of your office with excitement. If you get none, it is no big deal. You should be able to get one to three sponsors in the middle level and at least five to ten at the bottom level. If you do this, you will know that you have set your levels correctly.

 practical tip

Day of the Event

The day you have been planning for almost a year has finally arrived. Assign each board member to serve as greeters of VIP's and others who are new to the organization. Also assign someone to personally thank each sponsor.

A colleague recently told me that she color codes name tags so board members know who they are supposed to connect with and can find them easily. One board member is responsible for greeting people with blues nametags, another for green, another for red, etc.

The bottom line is that events should be fun! People should have a great feeling about your organization at the end of the event and want to come back year after year. Guests should also leave knowing more about your organization than when they arrived, without having been bored with long speeches. If you can do that, you have done your job well.

XYZ Organization
Sponsorship Form

Event Date and Time Location	Honorees and Speakers Listed Here Event Sponsors Listed Here

Name _____   Company Name _____

Address _____

Phone _____   Email _____

Sponsorship Opportunities

☐   Gold Sponsor $10,000
  ✓   Table of 10 (10 Tickets)
  ✓   Premium Full Page Ad in Program (back or inside covers)
  ✓   Name and Logo on Signage at Event
  ✓   Logo and Link on Website for One Year
  ✓   Name on Invitation (if committed by print deadline)

☐   Silver Sponsor $5,000
  ✓   Table of 10 (10 Tickets)
  ✓   Full Page Ad in Program
  ✓   Name and Logo on Signage at Event
  ✓   Name on Invitation (if committed by print deadline)

☐   Bronze Sponsor $2,500
  ✓   One Table of 10 (10 Tickets)
  ✓   Half Page Ad in Program

Journal Ads

☐ Full Page $X,XXX   ☐ Half Page Ad $XXX   ☐ Quarter Page $XXX

Please Make Checks Payable To: XYZ Organization

Name (on Credit Card) _____   Credit Card Number _____

Expiration Date _____   Security Code _____

Signature _____

Please Return Form To: XYZ Organization at Address of Organization

Questions? Please Call Susan at 123-456-7890

Follow-Up

If you were able to get important prospects to attend your event, then the follow-up could be the most important part of your event. Make sure you do not let too much time pass before reconnecting with these people, as they will still be glowing with good feelings about your organization. Call them quickly to schedule a tour of your facility or visit them at their home or office. Turn them into individual prospects if they

Count the number of personalized sponsorship solicitations you and your committee will make this year and add them to your list of asks for the year.

counting your asks

At any major event something will most likely go wrong. Stay calm. Getting hysterical or screaming at people does nothing to enhance the event or the situation. The following two examples show stressful event situations.

A few years ago, on the night before an event I was running, there was a thunder storm that knocked out the power to the entire area. The venue where the event was scheduled did not have power the day of the event. It rented generators the size of trucks, but did not have them up and running until thirty minutes before the guests arrived. The guests never knew there was a problem! If I had gotten angry or frustrated, it would have done nothing to improve the situation. Because of the hard-working staff at the venue, we had a happy result. Getting hysterical would not have changed the outcome.

Another time I hired a consultant to help me run an event. This consultant ended up screaming at the venue staff—in front of my guests! It did nothing to resolve the situation. You can be sure that I never hired that consultant again!

stories from the real world

Event Asks (Sponsorship)

	Prospect Name (Company/ Individual)	Committee Member Contact	Ask Amount	Response/ Amount
Example	Company XYZ	Jane Smith	$5,000	Yes/$2,500
1				
2				
3				
4				
5				
6				
7				
8				
9				
10				
11				
12				
13				
14				
15				

TOTAL REQUESTED: $ _____

TOTAL RECEIVED: $ _____

are not already part of your formal individual-giving plan. If they were at the event as part of your cultivation plan, do not lose event momentum by letting too much time pass before reconnecting with them.

To Recap

◆ Reasons to have events include: unrestricted dollars for your organization, opportunity to showcase your organization and build your database, and raise donations from those who might not otherwise give.

◆ Evaluate your events to determine if they are worth the time and expense you are putting into them.

◆ Develop a fundraising committee to sell sponsorships and tickets, not spend money to plan the event.

◆ Plan your events starting one year in advance.

◆ Follow up with VIP prospects who attend your event.

Chapter Seven

For Executive Directors Only

IN THIS CHAPTER

- ···➔ Understanding your role as chief fundraiser
- ···➔ Working with the board on fundraising
- ···➔ Recruiting and training board members
- ···➔ Supervising and working with your staff
- ···➔ How and when to hire your first development staff member
- ···➔ Screening resumes for good development skills
- ···➔ Interview questions and tips
- ···➔ Benefits and salary
- ···➔ First-year expectations

have included this chapter because it is my experience that executive directors generally do not have formal fundraising education or take advantage of continuing education opportunities. This chapter will speak directly to the experience of executive directors and fundraising. Some sections are directed at those executive directors who are doing it all themselves, and there are other sections aimed at those who are fortunate enough to have fundraising staff to work with. I will discuss how to work with your board and staff on fundraising and how each role is distinct.

The chapter continues with how and when to make the important decision of whether or not to hire your first development staff member. Many organizations agonize over the decision and process. I believe that in order to grow your organization, you need to get to a point where you and your board members are willing to take the next step in your organizational development and hire development staff. In this chapter I provide some tools to help make your decision, in addition to a sample job description and tips on how to screen and interview candidates. Finally, I will provide a brief section on salary and benefit guidelines, as well as developing reasonable expectations for year one.

Overcoming the Social Worker Mentality

If you took the path of so many executive directors, you might have started out as a direct service worker in your field: full of passion, creativity, and compassion. You might be a teacher, social worker, or other type of direct care worker, but over the years in order to get promotions you became a supervisor. Finally, whether you became an executive director by starting your own nonprofit or took the helm of an existing organization, you probably did so without much training in management or supervision, and most likely none in development (fundraising).

Now you are in the precarious position of doing all three: managing, supervising and fundraising. You might still pine for the days when you were in the trenches doing direct care work.

I hope this entire book, and particularly this chapter, will make your job a little easier and therefore more enjoyable and rewarding.

The Buck Stops Here—You are Responsible for Fundraising

If you have read this book in the order it is presented, you already know that you are critical to your organization's fundraising success.

If you skipped around or started with this chapter, it will become quickly apparent that fundraising should be a major component of your job responsibilities and your daily tasks as an executive director. This is true regardless of whether or not you have any fundraising staff.

If you are fortunate enough to have fundraising staff, fundraising is still a major part of your responsibilities. If you do not have any fundraising staff, then you are likely fully responsible for funds raised.

How to Get Your Board on Board

The most important thing about getting your board members on the fundraising bandwagon is to recruit them properly and set up realistic and honest expectations at the onset. It is unfair to get them on the board, then ambush them with expectations of giving and getting. If you do not establish expectations from the start, then you and the board member are bound to be disappointed.

Although the board is technically your boss, it is actually your responsibility as the executive director to manage the board.

I know executive directors who are so afraid of their boards that they let their board president or development chair run all over them. As executive director, it is your responsibility to guide and make recommendations to your board, while at the same time taking advantage of their expertise, experience and connections.

While the board/executive director relationship is a balancing act, it is important for the executive director to lead and guide the board and the organization.

practical tip

In an effort to change your board from a non-fundraising board to a fundraising board, not only is it important to recruit new board members, but it is also important to change the culture of the current board. If you previously operated with a non-fundraising board, it might take approximately three years or longer to have enough board turnover to really change the culture of your current board.

To open the hearts and minds (and wallets) of current board members, I look for one board member (a mole) with power and influence who tends to be supportive of a board fundraising effort. After a discussion of the situation and explanation of where I would like to see things go, I ask the member to speak with a few like-minded board members prior to a meeting where we will discuss the issue. The member will then lead a discussion on increased board participation with pre-planted supporters and slowly change the culture of the organization.

The reason that I have chosen to include this section in this chapter, rather than the chapter on board members, is that it is the job of the executive director to create and maintain a viable board. It is not the development director's job.

To help get off on the right foot with your new board members, have a pre-orientation/orientation packet that includes the following:

◆ Information about your organization including recent annual reports, newsletters, brochures, videos, etc.

◆ Organization history and mission.

◆ Budget.

◆ Bylaws.

◆ Strategic plan.

◆ Calendar of events and meetings.

◆ Board member job description.

◆ Board member expectation form.

◆ Board member conflict-of-interest form.

◆ Committee descriptions and expectations.

Sample Board Member Job Description

Board members of organization XYZ are expected to do the following:

◆ Be committed to the mission and cause of the organization.

◆ Attend and participate in meetings—both general board meetings and committee meetings. Two excused absences per year are allowed.

◆ Serve on at least one committee.

◆ Provide professional advice and expertise.

◆ Attend all special and fundraising events.

◆ Advocate on behalf of the organization.

◆ Make a personal contribution at a "stretch" level.

◆ Help with fundraising (see board member expectation form).

Board Member Expectation Form

In order to ensure that your board members fully understand what you expect of them, it is important to have a comprehensive board member expectation form. This concept and form can be introduced at a board meeting or retreat and then provided to all incoming board members. The form should be updated and filled out by each board member annually.

This form serves as a reminder of what the board member agrees to. It can be used when evaluating board member performance at the end of the year.

BOARD EXPECTATION FORM
(Sample)

Name: _____

As a board member, I understand my financial commitment is necessary to ensure the success of this organization.

My company and/or I will participate in the following ways this year:

___ Awards Dinner Sponsorships from ($5,000 - $10,000) $ _____

___ Golf Outing ($300/ticket+sponsorship opportunities) $_____

In order to achieve 100% participation of the board,
I personally pledge $ _____

TOTAL $ _____

For my personal gift, I would prefer to make:
___ One payment   ___Quarterly payments of $_____

___ My company will match my donation (I will submit the matching gift form with my payment(s)).

Please make gift or first pledge payment by March 1, so we can start the year with 100% participation.

As a board member, I agree to serve on 1 committee this year (please check):

___ Development Committee   ___ Finance Committee
___ Marketing/ Public Relations   ___ Nominating Committee

I understand that Board meeting attendance is key to the success of the Board and the agency and is a requirement for Board membership.

_____   _____
Board Member Signature   Date

Thank you very much for your commitment!

Team Approach: Working with Your Staff

I cannot emphasize enough the importance of working with your staff on fundraising. In the first chapters of this book I was often writing with the assumption that fundraising primarily falls to a single person, either the executive director or the director of development.

Now, I am going to break down the roles for the best case scenario, assume that everyone is working together and that you have a full, small-shop development team—executive director, development director, and administrative assistant. It is important to know the theory even if it does not always work in practice. It will give you something to strive for.

Role of the Executive Director

As executive director, you are the visionary and the "face" of your organization. You should be front and center with donors, as you are the one they want to meet and the one who can express best where the organization is headed.

Role of the Development Director

The director of development is responsible for:

◆ Helping to identify, cultivate, solicit and steward prospects.

◆ Creating a cultivation plan, which is generally executed by the executive director and a board member.

◆ Carrying out behind-the-scenes cultivation and facilitates meetings and next steps.

◆ Planning out the solicitation and doing any research involved with that process.

◆ The stewardship process.

I like to describe the role of you, the executive director, and your development director in the following way: You are the puppet and your development staff member is the puppeteer. The puppeteer does all behind-the-scenes work, and the puppet does all the entertaining. In other words, the director of development should fully prepare you to go out on stage.

Role of the Administrative Assistant

Administrative assistants, if you are fortunate enough to have one, are responsible for helping with generating thank-you letters, pre- and post-meeting letters, and scheduling appointments when appropriate.

I once worked with an organization that had a receptionist who was always grouchy. It came through loud and clear over the phone and in person. She treated people badly regardless of who they were—donors and board members included. Her attitude gave people a bad first impression of the organization. She was a real problem for the overall image of the agency, because all outsiders come in contact with her first.

In contrast, I recently went to a hospital to attend a committee meeting. There was a staff member in front of the information desk who not only gave me directions to the meeting room, but insisted on walking most of the way, down several hallways, with me. It was both shocking and incredibly gracious. It was a wonderfully welcoming way to enter the hospital and made quite an impression on me.

The hospital staff and policies turned what could have been a "non-experience," finding a meeting room, or potentially a bad experience, if I had gotten lost or frustrated, into a positive and memorable one.

While these might seem like minor incidents, they could mean the difference between a gift from a donor and no gift.

The administrative assistant is generally the first person that people contacting your organization come in contact with. Their interaction with the administrative assistant is important to the overall "vibe" of the organization.

Everyone needs to be involved in making friends for the organization, as is illustrated in the "stories from the real world" sidebar.

Supervising Your Development Staff

I know many well-meaning executive directors who are so overwhelmed with management and other responsibilities that they leave the fundraising to the director of development. There are several problems with this approach. First, the development director cannot raise as much money alone as could be raised with your involvement. Second, many development directors, especially less experienced ones, need benchmarks and supervision to stay on track.

It is important that you work closely with your development director, and hold the person accountable for getting asks out the door. Without micromanaging, have a list of goals and accomplishments for the development director to "check-off" each month and follow up to make sure things are getting crossed off the list.

This entire book was designed and written because too many small development shops are not asking or raising nearly as much as they could, or should. It is up to you to ensure that the fundraising process is being followed for all prospects, and that your schedule of asks is getting followed.

Knowing When to Hire Your First Development Staff Member

There comes a time in the life of every nonprofit when it is time to hire the first development staff member. How do you know when it's time to do so? While there is no clear cut answer to this important question, there are several important factors to consider:

◆ Why do you want to hire a development staff member? If it is so you do not need to fundraise any more, that is not a good answer.

Hopefully your organization has grown to the point that you can afford an additional staff member and are ready to grow your programs and services, which will require additional funding.

◆ Do you have the funding to pay the first year's salary? Organizations that expect development staff to immediately raise their own salary (generally unrestricted operating dollars) have unrealistic expectations from the start and are setting up the new staff member for failure. It is reasonable and expected that increased revenue will be generated in the first year, but it is unlikely that it will be enough unrestricted dollars to cover the cost of a salary and benefits for your new staff member.

◆ Have you discussed this new position with the board? The development committee should expect to work with the development staff member. If there is no development committee of the board, one of the first tasks for the new staff member will be to create one.

◆ Who will the new staff member report to?

It is my strong belief that your top development staff member (or only development staff member, in this case) should report to the executive director. This is because you will want to work closely together on fundraising. The only exception to this might be if you decide to hire a grant writer, who will not be working on any other types of fundraising.

Going from One to Two Development Staff

When you get to the point of needing a second development staff member, it is probably because you are ready to grow in a particular area, such as grants or individual giving. There are many ways to grow your development office, and much of the decision will be based on the talents and skills already in your development shop. Some organizations might want to consider their second development staff member as a grant writer, event planner, or major gifts director.

Determining the Right Person for Your Office

Before creating a job description and starting your search for the perfect candidate, you will want to determine what type of person you are looking for. If your salary scale is small, you might want to consider someone straight from college who is eager, enthusiastic, hard working and willing to learn on the job. If you are seeking someone with more experience, you will need to be prepared to pay a higher salary.

The next question to answer is: Do you want a generalist with small-shop experience, or do you want someone with major gifts skills? If your current program staff can handle the grant writing and event planning, you might want to consider someone who will grow your individual giving program.

There is rarely the perfect person with the exact experience and skill set that you are looking for. However, there are often several people with many of the skills and personality traits that you would like. Review resumes and interview candidates with an open mind. See the sample job description on page 119 to get started with your search.

Schedule weekly meetings with your development team, whoever that might be. It could be you and your development staff member, plus the administrative assistant if appropriate. If you do not have any staff to help with development, schedule a weekly meeting with your board president or development committee.

The meeting does not have to be longer than fifteen minutes and will have the same two agenda items each week:

◆ What ask did we make last week and how did it go?

◆ What ask is coming up, what still needs to be done to prepare, who is going to do it, and who will make the ask or get it out the door?

Someone in one of my seminars once suggested that you hold the meeting standing up to keep from getting sidetracked, so that the meeting does not last longer than the allotted fifteen minutes!

to-do lists

Sample Job Description

When preparing your first development job description, take advantage of existing job descriptions from similar organizations to get appropriate language and reasonable requirements and qualifications. You can find these on any job search site.

Advertising Your Development Position

The most appropriate place to advertise a development position is in whatever publication or website most development people in your area look for jobs. Examples include:

◆ Association of Fundraising Professionals which can be found at: jobs.afpnet.org. $275 for 30 days online.*

◆ CharityChannel which can be found at charitychannel.com. $127 for 120 days online.*

◆ *Chronicle of Philanthropy* which can be found at: philanthropy.com/jobs. $175 for 30 days online.*

◆ Idealist which can be found at www.idealist.org. $60 per job.*

Rates in effect at the time of publication.

Screening Resumes

While how to screen resumes might seem obvious to you if you have done lots of hiring, if you have never hired a development person before it is important to know what to look for. Some of the points would apply to any type of position.

◆ Prior development experience.
As basic as this is, I have received many resumes for development positions where the applicant has no prior development experience. If you are hiring someone straight from college, this is alright, but not if you are looking for someone with experience.

XYZ Nonprofit Organization

Job Title: Director of Development
Job Location: New York, New York

Organization Description:
XYZ Organization has served homeless women and children in NYC for the last ten years. We are ready to hire our first development staff member and are looking for a terrific candidate to join our team.

Responsibilities Include:
◆ Creating initial development office.
◆ Working with executive director to establish development plan and goals.
◆ Researching and identifying funding opportunities including foundations, corporations, and individuals.
◆ Reaching or exceeding annual fundraising goals.
◆ Overseeing all administrative functions related to development, including data entry and data management, letter generation, etc.
◆ Working with board members and board committees including development committee and events committees.

Salary & Benefits:
◆ Salary is negotiable and based on experience.
◆ Generous benefits package with healthcare and days off.

Qualifications:
◆ Bachelors Degree required, Master's Degree preferred.
◆ CFRE preferred.
◆ Experience in a one-person development shop preferred.
◆ Proven track record of fundraising with grant writing, events, and individual campaigns.
◆ Excellent interpersonal and writing skills.

How to Apply:
◆ Send cover letter and resume to: Joan Jones at XYZ at jjones@xyz.org.
◆ No phone calls please.

This is an easy elimination point. If they don't have it, they don't have it.

◆ Duration at prior jobs.
Does the individual have staying power or does the applicant bounce from job to job? If the candidate switches jobs every year or eighteen months, it is a red flag. Any short-term (less than eighteen months) position should be asked about in an interview. If there are more than one or two, it is a real concern.

◆ Promotions and increasingly more responsibility with matching titles.
A very positive sign on a resume is when a person has received one or more promotions at a job or has had various jobs with increased levels of responsibility.

◆ The types of organizations that the person has worked for.
For example, if the applicant has worked at only arts organizations, and your organization is a homeless shelter, you might want to discuss why the candidate wants to work in this new area and find out the person's level of commitment to your cause. In order to be an effective fundraiser, the person must be genuinely interested in the mission.

Interviewing for Development Staff

Remember to ask open ended questions and think about the candidate from the perspective of the donor.

◆ *Do you want this person representing your organization to donors?*

◆ *Will this person fit with the culture of your organization?*

◆ *Is the candidate friendly? Does the person smile?*

◆ *Is the candidate a team player?*

Sample interview questions are:

◆ *Why are you interested in this position?*

◆ *What experience in your background makes you qualified for this job?*

◆ *Why are you leaving your current position? If there are lots of positions on the person's resume, ask about why they left other jobs.*

◆ *Tell me about your development experience.*

◆ *How have you raised money in the past—events, grant writing, individuals, direct mail, etc.?*

◆ *What fundraising have you done that was successful and what not as successful? Why do you think one campaign was successful and the other not?*

◆ *What would you require to be successful at your job?*

◆ *Have you been involved in any continuing education? Are you interested in continuing education?*

◆ *How do you envision working with me (the executive director) in this position?*

◆ *Have you worked with a board or development committee before? In what capacity?*

◆ *What do you expect from board members? How would you work with them?*

Salary and Benefits

Of course there is a wide range of salary and benefits offered from organization to organization, depending on the size and budget of the organization, the type of services provided, and region of the country that the organization is located in.

The Association of Fundraising Professionals (AFP) does an annual salary survey, which is probably the most useful reference when starting out. The amount you need to pay will largely depend on how much prior fundraising experience you are looking for, what industry you are in, and where you are located. For example, if you plan to hire someone without any prior experience straight out of college, you will not need to pay nearly as much as if you want someone with a Certified Fund Raising Executive (CFRE) credential who has been in the field for five or more years. Likewise, if your organization is in New York City, you will be paying a higher salary than if you are located in South Dakota.

For whatever nonprofits lack in salary, they can often provide other types of compensation, such as days off. These benefits also vary widely from organization to organization, but since this is something you can offer without additional funding, I think it is an important place to be generous. Days off help people recharge their mental batteries, and often help with morale. I believe that a minimum of four weeks of vacation time will often substitute for a lower salary. Whenever possible, give people time off around the winter holidays or by closing early on Fridays during the summer as an added bonus.

Other possible benefits, depending on your HR policies, include health insurance, retirement plans, sick days and other perks.

What to Expect from the First Year

There is an extremely high turnover rate among development professionals. I believe one of the reasons that this is the case is that executive directors have unrealistic expectations of what development staff can accomplish, especially with the tools and resources that they are given. A new development staff member will raise money in the first year, but is not likely to bring in the position's salary in unrestricted dollars. The development staff member might bring in grant dollars that amount to more than the position's salary, but are likely to be program dollars that cannot be spent on administrative salary.

Set expectations at the onset, so you have something to measure success against at the end of the first year. For year one, some examples of good goals include:

◆ Establish a board development committee and meet six times. Create goals for board members.

◆ Work with board members to give and get. Have a plan to achieve 100 percent participation.

◆ Research and apply for eight to ten new grants. Establish relationships with foundation staff members.

◆ Plan one event with a minimum of one hundred guests, which raises $15,000 or more. Follow up with VIP's from the event.

◆ Plan two house parties for prospective donors at the homes of board members.

◆ Send two new mailings to database.

◆ Create capacity for electronic correspondence and send five e-blasts.

◆ Help identify ten individual prospects and create cultivation plans for each. Help schedule meetings with them to meet board members and the executive director.

These are some examples of reasonable first-year goals without unreasonable expectations of raising specific dollar amounts.

Budget Before You Hire

In addition to salary and benefits, you will want to provide the resources that a development staff member needs to succeed. This means that there must be a budget for development activities. For example, what activities do you expect the new staff member to implement? Extra mailings cost money. Events cost money. Databases cost money. The expression "it takes money to make money" applies here. If you do not have a budget for your development staff member, you cannot expect this person to implement many new fundraising activities or raise much money.

To Recap

◆ Executive directors are ultimately responsible for fundraising for their organizations.

◆ Well-trained and selected board members will serve their organizations better than untrained board members.

◆ Board members need clear expectations, orientation, and ongoing training.

◆ All staff members can help with advocacy and fundraising.

◆ Each staff member has an important role in fundraising.
◆ Supervision is critical for success.

◆ Know when to hire your first development staff member.

◆ Recruit, interview, and hire your first development staff member.

◆ Create realistic expectations for your development staff member.

Chapter Eight

Putting it All Together: Keys to Success

IN THIS CHAPTER

- ····→ Measuring success
- ····→ Setting goals and sticking to them
- ····→ Staying on track
- ····→ Strategies for staying motivated

A s you know by now, *50 Asks in 50 Weeks* is about creating a simple development plan for busy small offices. However, if the plan is not used by the people who created it, then it is not worth the paper it is written on. This final chapter outlines how to stay on track, follow your plan, and count and measure your success.

Creating Goals and Objectives

Most people who use *50 Asks in 50 Weeks* have the same goal: to raise more money. As I have discussed throughout this book, you can accomplish this goal by asking for gifts more frequently and asking in smarter, more efficient ways. To narrow down the overarching goal of raising more money you will want to develop specific goals and objectives.

Goals are general and broad in scope and objectives are more specific. When creating goals, write them down and refer back to them monthly or quarterly to make sure you are on track. For each goal, list several objectives that will help you meet that goal, the staff or board member who is responsible for making it happen, and a deadline.

Sample Goals and Objectives

Goal 1: Increase board participation in fundraising.

Objectives	Responsible Party	Deadline
100% participation	Board President	February 1st
2 board f/r trainings	Development Dir.	March and Sept

Goal 2:   Enhance bulk solicitation program.

Objectives	Responsible Party	Deadline
Send 1 new mail appeal	Development Dir.	March
Send 4 e-newsletters	Development Dir.	Quarterly
Add notes to top donor appeals	Executive Director	October/March

Duplicate this chart or create your own system of listing your goals and objectives. Keep it simple enough to follow and refer back to frequently. Goals and objectives are important, so that you know where you want to go and have a way of knowing when you have gotten there. Review your goals and objectives annually. If you did not accomplish one or more of them, it will be critical to examine the reason why.

Creating Your Fundraising Plan and Staying on Track

After completing all of the worksheets in this book, you should be able to condense a summary of your fifty asks onto a one-page worksheet. The worksheet on the following page is a single page snapshot of the asks you will make in the coming year.

50 Asks in 50 Weeks Summary Sheet (on following page)

Fill in each box with the name of a prospect or solicitation such as individual, corporation, foundation, bulk mail solicitation, etc., and the staff member who is responsible for the ask. All worksheets in this book are available for free on my website for downloading and printing at www.tripointfundraising.com.

The only way I know of to truly keep on track and focused is by being accountable to someone else and setting public deadlines for yourself. As I mentioned in the beginning of this book, schedule weekly development meetings with another person in your office, either the executive director, development director, board president or development committee chair, or the administrative assistant. The only two agenda items for this weekly meeting are, first, reviewing last week's ask and, second, discussing upcoming asks. Knowing that you will need to report on your progress to someone else will really light a fire under you like nothing else. It will also keep you accountable.

Measuring Success

There are many ways to measure success. The first and most obvious is the total number of dollars raised. However, there are many other measures and factors to consider in addition to the bottom line. For example:

50 Asks in 50 Weeks Summary Sheet

	Week 1 (1st Ask)	Week 2 (2nd Ask)	Week 3 (3rd Ask)	Week 4 (4th Ask)	5th Ask (Optional)
Example	*M. Smith ED/ Bd. Mbr.*	*Ford Grant DOD*	*Gala Invites DOD*	*Bank Sponsor Request Bd. Mbr.*	*E-mail Newsletter DOD*
January					
February					
March					
April					
May					
June					
July					
August					
September					
October					
November					
December					

◆ Number of new donors.
Know the number of donors to any given campaign. How many people donated to your fall appeal this year and last year? How many came to your event?

◆ Average gift size?
Pay attention to the average gift size—does it rise or fall from year to year?

◆ Number of grants received.
It is not simply the number of foundations you apply to but the number of grants you actually receive that is important.

◆ Percentage of renewal donors/retention rate.
Acquisition of new donors costs more than keeping old donors. Measure and track how many donors you renew and those you lose from year to year.

Staying Motivated

Staying motivated and positive is the number one way I know to be a truly successful fundraiser. Negativity becomes a self-fulfilling prophesy. In other words, if you believe that you won't raise any money, and then you act like you won't raise any money by sitting around moping at your desk, then you actually won't raise any money. On the other hand, if you truly believe that you will raise money and act like it by going out and meeting with prospects and donors, the money will follow.

One of the most frustrating parts of being in a one-person development shop for me was the feeling of isolation and loneliness with regard to other professionals who were engaged in the type of work I was doing. Yes, I was surrounded by social workers, but I did not have anyone to bounce my fundraising ideas off of. If you can, find a colleague or friend at another agency to help keep you motivated. Schedule a weekly pep talk and bounce questions off each other. If your conversations start to get negative, find another friend.

The board president of an organization I work with told me an amazing story. She was in line at the grocery store and recognized the woman in front of her as a parent at her daughter's school. As they approached the front of the line, the woman realized that she had forgotten her wallet. Seeing that she only had a few items, the board president offered to pay for her items and gave her a $20 bill, knowing that she would probably never see the money again. She didn't have any paper on her to write down her name and phone number, but had a generic card from the organization and scribbled her name on that. A week went by and the board president had forgotten all about it when she received a call from the executive director of her organization who told her that there was a letter for her with a $20 bill in cash and a $200 check for the organization!

The Association of Fundraising Professionals has provided me with a fantastic network of professionals to consult and debrief with. Find a group of fundraisers in your area to meet with or speak to on a regular basis.

Wrapping Up

Final Asking Ideas

- ◆ Ask the board.

- ◆ Ask your clients.

- ◆ Ask your volunteers.

- ◆ Ask the board members to ask their friends, family, neighbors, and colleagues.

- Ask the staff to ask their friends, family and neighbors.

- Ask on your website.

- Ask in fall, spring, summer, and winter newsletters.

- Ask by bulk mail in a year-end appeal and throughout the year.

- Ask in monthly or quarterly electronic appeals.

- Ask in person, on the phone and by mail.

- Ask on social networks—Facebook, LinkedIn, Twitter.

- Ask your vendors to be sponsors and supporters.

- Ask, ask and ask some more!

I hope you have now identified at least fifty new prospects for your organization and learned a few new tips on smart and frequent fundraising. If you implement ideas learned in this book, I encourage you to contact me to let me know what is working in your shop, as well as what is not. I want to hear from you if you raise more money and even if you do not.

Good luck for a prosperous year in fundraising!

To Recap

- Set goals and objectives to raise more money.

- Stay motivated and positive about fundraising.

- Measure your success in order to know how you are doing.

- Work with others in your office on a weekly basis to keep on track.

- Ask, ask, and ask some more.

Appendix

Glossary

Acquisition refers to the number of new donors you have each year. For example, if an organization has 1,000 donors and 100 of those are new donors each year, then 10 percent of their donor base is acquisitions.

An **Ask** is the solicitation in the fundraising process. I will use the term to refer to any request for money, including a grant application, event invitation, appeal letter, sponsorship request or an individual, face-to-face solicitation.

Bulk solicitations/bulk mail/direct mail will refer to traditional (snail mail) or electronic solicitations. **Bulk** means that multiple people will be asked for a donation within the same solicitation (appeal letter or e-mail).

Capacity refers to individuals and whether or not they have the means (or ability) to make a gift.

A **Case Statement** is a written statement about why your organization is important, worthy and deserves donations.

Cultivation is the process where prospects and organizations get to know one another. In other words, board and staff members educate prospects about the organization, and board and staff get to know the prospect.

Cultivation takes place over a period of time and can last from a few months to several years, prior to asking for a gift.

Diversified Funding Base is having multiple revenue streams coming from a variety of sources.

Give and Get refers to board members and it means give money, (and) get money or get off the board.

Identification is the first stage of the fundraising cycle. This is the stage where prospective donors are identified as potential donors.

Inclination measures whether or not individuals are philanthropically minded, and have an interest in your organization or cause. High inclination indicates a high level of interest in your organization.

Lapsed donors are donors who have stopped giving—in other words, former donors. This is generally measured within a year and someone is considered lapsed if they have not given in the last twelve months.

One Hundred Percent Participation refers to your board and the number of board members who are giving to your organization. All board members must contribute for your board to achieve 100 percent participation.

A **Prospect** is an individual, foundation or corporation that has been identified as a potential donor to your organization.

Retention refers to the number of donors you are able to keep from year to year. What percentage and number of donors are you keeping (or retaining) from year to year?

A **Soft Ask** is an indirect request for donations. For example, a soft ask could be a reply envelope included in a newsletter. The main point of the newsletter is not a direct request for a donation, as it would be in an appeal letter, yet the request is still there in the form of the reply envelope.

Solicitation is the actual ask or request for funding, and is what most people think of when they hear about fundraising. I will use the term to refer to any request for money including a grant application, event invitation, appeal letter, sponsorship request, or an individual or face-to-face request. Solicitations can happen in person, by mail, by application or by phone.

Stewardship is the thanking or follow-up stage of the fundraising cycle. After a gift is made it is important to properly steward donors.

A **Stretch Gift** is a gift of any amount that is large for that particular donor's giving ability. When a person is considering a stretch gift, it is a contribution that the person needs to think seriously about before giving and not one that the donor can easily write a check for. It is often a gift of a sizeable enough amount that the donor would discuss it with a spouse or family member, prior to giving the gift.

Index

C

Just Released!

FUNDRAI$ING
as a Career

What, Are You Crazy?

www.charitychannel.com